CHOOSING
RESEARCH
METHODS

DATA COI
FOR DEVELOPM

Development Guidelines No. 7

Brian Pratt and Peter Loizos

A catalogue record for this book is available from the British Library.

ISBN 0 85598 176 8 Hardback
ISBN 0 85598 177 6 Paperback

This book is dedicated to our development partners, GMS and JBP.

PL and BP

Published by Oxfam, 274 Banbury Road, Oxford OX2 7DZ
Designed by Oxfam Design Unit
Printed by Oxfam Print Unit

CONTENTS

FOREWORD

This book started life in a 'brainstorming' workshop in which the following people took part: Dr Jo Boyden, Roy Cole, Donnacadh Hurley, Dr Peter Loizos, Dr David Marsden, Anne Muir, Dr Brian Pratt, Dr Allan Stanton, Roy Trivedy, and Dr Tina Wallace. The ideas of the group were then written up by Brian Pratt and Peter Loizos.

The book is intended as an introduction to research for small-scale development programmes. It will not make you instantly proficient in any of the methods described, but it should help you to decide what sort of research you might do, and what the advantages and disadvantages are of particular methods. So it should guide you to a choice of methods, and prepare you to go deeper into the methods of your choosing.

If you have taken a course in Social Research Methods, this book will be probably be too introductory for you. It is designed to complement other volumes in the *Development Guidelines* series. Once many of the questions posed here have been answered, the reader may well decide that (for example) a full-scale survey is required. *Development Guidelines 6, Social Survey Methods: A fieldguide for development workers*, by Paul Nichols, gives a full explanation of methodology for carrying out surveys with limited resources. Number five in the series is *Evaluating Social Development Projects*, edited by David Marsden and Peter Oakley, and this, too, may prove helpful. We have, for the most part, assumed for the purposes of this book that research is a part of the project cycle; however, we have not specifically considered the different elements of that cycle and their needs.

Throughout, we have tried to concentrate on a small numberof well-tried methods, rather than provide a catalogue including all minor ones. For example, we have not discussed the 'logical framework' approach in any depth, because it is a way of organising the data collection rather than a separate method of collecting it. (Appendix 4 outlines the principles of logical framework analysis.)

Inevitably, one method tends to overlap with another, so some degree of repetition has been unavoidable. We have also been concerned to present the issues in an accessible way rather than to pursue them in all their technical complexity. There are references to other useful books for the reader who wishes to get deeper into particular methods or issues.

The authors would like to express their thanks to all the participants in the original group workshop. The book would not have been possible without the experience and ideas they contributed. Peter Loizos would like to thank Paddy Barwise, Martin Bulmer, Robert Dodd and John Harriss for their most helpful comments.

INTRODUCTION

This guide is about research which is action-linked, that is, tied to some form of practical intervention. By 'research' we mean no more than the systematic collection, analysis and dissemination of information. Research might be carried out in response to a request by a local group to help them meet some problem, or to help a funding agency determine its priorities or, later on, to assist the planning and operation of a specific project. The research may be tied to feasibility studies for a proposed programme, monitoring and evaluation of an ongoing programme or alternatively to the final evaluation of a programme which has ended.

One argument of this book is that research should be integrated into the programme cycle and not be set apart as an activity carried out by people unfamiliar with the programme. A second contention is that there is no perfect research model which can be used for all situations: to be effective, research must be tailored to fit the specific problem. A third assumption is that gender-related questions should be raised for most if not all research projects, at all stages of research — initial formulation, research design, data collection, and analysis. And a final assumption is that responsible and sensitive research is always conducted consultatively, together with the people affected, rather than inflicted upon them from above, or outside.

The word 'research' should not conjure up some very difficult and specialised activity which can only be done by people with higher degrees. We all do research with a small 'r' constantly, since we collect information in our daily lives and use it to guide our decisions. Sometimes, however, we need to consult people with special skills to help us in this process, such as engineers, surveyors, accountants, health specialists of many kinds, just as nobody trying to offer an especially delicious meal would think twice about reaching for a cookery book. But the more we learn for ourselves the skills for which we sometimes turn to experts, the better placed we are to pursue our goals and to evaluate the contributions of specialists. Research with a capital 'R' is a systematic approach to the gathering of information to solve specific problems — no more, but no less. It is the **systematic** character, the desire to eliminate errors, which marks out serious research from normal problem solving.

Attitudes to development are undergoing continuous change, and in the last 20 years or so there has been a major change in thinking on several related issues: first, to what extent is a development programme one which has developed in close response to the expressed needs of a local group, and how far should it remain the brain-child of planners and policy makers at several removes from the group in question? Put in another way, this asks whether experts are serving the local people or are prisoners of their own interests and disciplines. Thus, 'expert-driven' research has been called into question, and the idea is gaining ground that the best development research both begins and ends with the expressed needs of local groups who will be most crucially affected by it. Experts should be on tap, but not on top.

The second issue involves the political values which underpin an agency's involvement with a local group. How fully is the agency consultative, democratic, and sensitive to local perceptions and wishes? 'Top-down' development programmes are often accompanied by research which is insensitive towards the very people it is supposedly meant to assist. It is therefore increasingly the case that research is carried out in closer collaboration with the people affected, using their knowledge, skills and, where this is their wish their energies; and at the very least in a way which gives them as strong a voice as they think they want about what research is planned, why it is planned, and how it might proceed.

The third issue concerns the nature of expertise itself. In the period before the first atomic bomb was dropped upon Hiroshima, there was a general optimism about science in all the industrial countries and among the leaders of independence movements. Science and social science were then perceived as expert systems which would solve most human problems within

2

a foreseeable future, and people who had not received any kind of scientific training tended to have their knowledge downgraded. Since 1945 this optimism has been challenged by a far more balanced view of scientific 'progress', and a gradual reduction in what might be called the misplaced over-valuing of experts. It is now increasingly realised that in many matters, from local medicines and local knowledge of animals, plants, crops, and the environment, to local scepticism about the market, money, and profit-taking, the understandings of small-scale pre-literate societies are often as pertinent as the most up-to-date scientific thinking, and often a good deal more environmentally sensitive. In the past, scientists and policy makers have backed many ideas which have later been shown to be dangerously wrong, and we are in the process of trying to find a new balance in our appraisal of the very nature of knowledge about the world, a balance which will no longer overvalue formal, official science and undervalue indigenous knowledge.

Since neither experts nor locals are always right, or always wrong, the process of readjusting the relation between the two will be slow and, in a conflict between different kinds of knowledge, it may often be hard to decide which view is the most worthwhile.

We hope that these three issues have sufficiently informedthe arguments in this book. We believe that there is no politically correct, off-the-peg answer to the questions raised by these debates, and that the issues can only be decided on a case-by-case, trial-and-error basis. There is no substitute for discussion and consultation, nor for judgement and balance.

3

1 STARTING RESEARCH: SOME BASIC ISSUES

Identifying a research need

Research never 'just happens' — it is always started by some person or interest group, with a problem or policy goal. Sometimes, the very decision to call for research will be hotly debated within a community or an agency, for research will certainly involve energy, time and money. However, it is also commonly the case that there are differences of opinion within an agency about whether a particular programme should be undertaken or not, or if it is going well or badly; and such divergent views may result in disagreements over whether research is needed, or what its focus should be. The initial definition of a research 'problem' is therefore a matter to be carefully thought through.

Sometimes the most important question may go unasked: has the problem initially identified by the funding agency the same degree of importance to the people the programme or policy is intended to benefit? What preconceptions are at work which might be rejected as meaningless by the people concerned? For example, some approaches to street children have assumed that their problems are that they have been abandoned by their parents and by society — but the children themselves often define their problems differently, in less passive terms, stressing their wish to make better livings for themselves. In another instance, well-meaning visitors to Cairo were outraged by the working conditions of the people known as Zabballeen, who live by sifting through the rubbish dumps of the city. The result was an inappropriate aid programme to change the living conditions for this group without any understanding of the economic and social relations within it. The programme was a failure, because the basic research had not been done, and the primary assumptions of the outsiders had not been questioned.

Specialists of various kinds tend to view groups of people through the lenses of their own specialisms. Water engineers worry particularly about people using dirty water and having poor sanitation, and health workers become preoccupied with disease and nutritional inadequacies. In such cases, the major problem may be defined in terms of the 'specialty', although a sensitive researcher, asking the people themselves to name their biggest problems, might well hear not about disease or water but about land tenure or loss of income. Thus, the questions must always be asked — who says this problem is the **major** problem facing the community, and what priority do **the people themselves** give it?

Traditionally, one group has dominated the identification of development issues to be researched: white, middle-class, middle-aged males. Although this situation is changing, it explains why some areas of society and the economy have received significant attention over the years whilst other areas have been consistently neglected. Typically, this has often meant that women's interests have been disregarded. To take the simplest example: a community may be unanimous about the desire for an improved well to be dug. If only a few senior men are consulted about the siting of the well, it may be dug in a place which inflicts a burden on women as the people who most commonly carry the water from the well to the home. There is now more research being done which is initiated and directed by women, but it is still rare for lower-class groups to initiate development research, and children almost never do so.

There are a number of phases of a development project or programme at which the need for systematic research might be identified. First, the **feasibility study:** if a community or group request an input from an agency, the potential funders are faced with the question, should we try to meet this request? Is this a problem which our policies allow us to address? What is to be done about this, by what means, on what scale? If a major disaster or emergency is in progress, some assessment of basic needs will be needed to inform the intervention. The most important things to find out will be the numbers of people affected, and their social profile — how many men, women, and children, at what ages, with what skills, and resources, and with what cultural requirements concerning, for example, diet. The feasibility study is perhaps the most important single piece of research which project planners can do, because the basic issues about the appropriateness and the future viability of the project should be tackled at this stage. some agencies are increasing the time-depth of their involvement. Action Aid, for example, now seeks to work in a defined geographical area for not less than ten years, and requires its staff to examine three separate areas in detail before committing the agency to one of them.

Research might be required at the **project planning** stage. Assuming that it has now been established what service or input a local group desire, this phase focuses on how it might best be delivered and administered. The research might be directed to finding out who owns which resources, and under what terms a necessary input such as a plot of land might be made available to the project. Questions of responsibility for the local running of the project would also need to be raised and decided. In such a situation, research, consultation, and planning of project administration are a single, continuous process, with the agency's representative inquiring as effectively as possible into how the beneficiaries conceive of their participation, and making clear to them the policy considerations which will guide the agency in deciding whether or not to fund the proposed project. At the planning stage, future monitoring and evaluation research could be designed to ensure periodically that the project was continuing to meet its stated goals. Best practice should seek to specify how the alleviation of poverty will be demonstrated. That is, the measurement of changes of income, consumption, and well-being should be planned at an early stage.

If the project has been in operation for some time, research as part of the process of **monitoring and evaluation** will be valuable in making clear to all concerned just how far the original needs are being met. Supposing a revolving fund for small loans to assist in income-generation projects for marginal groups has been in operation. Since the viability of the scheme in the middle and long term will depend on the loan repayments of the initial recipients, some analysis of the records will be essential.

Such an analysis is research with a small 'r'. It can obviously be carried out in two quite different ways. On the one hand, the senior agency staff manager could look at the records and draw out their implications. Or, if the scheme is very much under the control of a local group, the recipients of the loans could be invited to participate in the data-analysis phase, so that they all learned together just how well or badly the project was meeting its goals.

Finally, there is **retrospective evaluation research**, which is intended to reveal exactly why a project worked or did not work in a particular way. This type of research could involve analysis of project documents, interviews with all relevant participants, and comparisons with projects in other places which had started with similar goals and faced similar problems.

The level of participation

In recent years the development research community has become concerned about the possibility that traditional research procedures are perceived by local groups as intrusive, aggressive, and distanced, and that too much development planning has been a top-down affair, carried out in the name of local welfare but over the heads of local people. To counter this, an idea of development planning and linked research has arisen which is altogether more consultative and collaborative.

For these and other reasons approaches have been developed which have a completely different style and rationale. Hence, the idea of 'participatory' research, in which researcher and local people collaborate closely to explore the issues which the locals think require research and action. The research is not something initiated by the outside researchers, directed and controlled by them, but rather something which grows up more naturally and organically from the perceptions of the community, and their co-option of the researchers. And even where an outside researcher makes an initial overture, the subsequent course of the relationship need not be outsider-led. But all kinds of compromises are possible: if outsiders propose a project, and the local people show enthusiasm, the subsequent direction of the work can still be largely determined by their ideas and interests.

Although some writers make it sound as though there is a separate 'participatory' research method, this is misleading. The idea of participation is more an overall guiding philosophy of how to proceed, than a selection of specific methods. So when people talk about participatory research, participatory monitoring and participatory evaluation, on the whole they are not discussing a self-contained set of methodologies, but a situation whereby the methods being used have included an element of strong involvement and consultation on the part of the subjects of the research. Not all methods or groups are equally amenable to participation. For example, some of the technical methods described later can only be carried out and interpreted after a lengthy training, and although anyone might undergo such a training, it is usually the case that the research is needed now, rather than in several years' time.

We must retain a critical and sometimes sceptical view of processes described as participatory, particularly because many national governments compel their citizens to take part in development programmes. The word 'participation' has been usedby enthusiastic practitioners to include anything from obligatory, through to genuinely democratic and enthusiastic, involvement in a research project. Participation should be empowering, not merely a process whereby people co-operate without complaint.

A sense of the extent of participation can be had by reviewing the number of stages at which local people are involved in the research process. Does participation occur at all stages of the research (design, collection of data, interpretation, discussion and presentation) or only at certain points in the process? And if it does not occur at all stages, is the local community really disadvantaged by this? How busy are they? Do they really want to be involved at every phase of research, given that they may have crops to weed, children to feed, fuel and water to find, and dozens of other daily tasks? Perhaps their participation should be strategic, rather than total? About the big issues, rather than the nuts-and-bolts?

Where there are limitations on the degree of participation, is this for unavoidable technical reasons, or because the researchers want to maintain their exclusive control over the process and data collected? That is one of the more important questions to be considered. Imagine how you would react to a

9

group of people who arrived in your neighbourhood saying that they had a scheme for improving the quality of your life, but requesting you to stop whatever you normally do, and take part in a week-long exercise reviewing the neighbourhood's resources through a large-scale house-to-house census. You might well suppose that you know enough about these matters not to wish to give so much of your time to such a project.

It is important to establish at an early stage the nature of the research participation expected and desired. Unrealistic expectations should not be encouraged. It is important to establish whether participation will go as far as allowing the subjects overall decision-making power or whether you intend to reserve some decisions. By involving people in genuine power-sharing exercises they can be indirectly empowered through widening their access to information, and by being encouraged to express their views.

Recent experience has shown that, where it has been well-managed, participatory research can in itself be an empowering process. It can assist a group to work through questions, issues, and future possibilities. It can help them to improve their understanding of the society and culture in which they live and the alternatives open to them. At a more mundane level it can help a group establish priorities for action in very practical ways.

Perhaps the most serious question to ask before initiating a particular style of research is in what ways the community will benefit from the exercise. Suppose you are trying to decide between full continuous power-sharing participation, or a form which involves the beneficiaries in less intensive involvement. If the target group are people with time on their hands, little self-confidence, and a need to feel that they can act effectively (e.g. a group of unemployed young people), then a fully consultative, fully participatory research project might do something significant to enhance their self-esteem and skills, and thus become genuinely empowering. But to ask a group of women, who are already struggling with child care and the management of farms because their men are away working as migrant labourers, to devote precious time to step-by-step research participation might be to ask too much of them. They will be able to advise you on this, and you need to be sensitive to nuances here. They may wish to show enthusiasm for the project and, in hope of your agency's financial support, may be ready to say that they can devote time and energy to research. It will be the way they say this — whether eagerly, or with a marked lack of enthusiasm — which will suggest how they perceive the task ahead. This will need to be discussed sensitively and in detail with them, so that a realistic assessment can be jointly agreed.

Community self-diagnosis: One simple system for community diagnosis entailed a community meeting together and listing major health problems in their area (respiratory disease, TB, skin infections, intestinal problems). The group then listed separately possible solutions (build a health post, introduce piped water, organise rubbish collection). The two lists were then the focus of group discussions about how the solutions might or might not improve the health of the community. The results showed that often the most obvious or commonly stated solution, in this case 'build a health post', was not necessarily the most effective, or the least expensive, way of improving health in the community. Instead, to improve water supplies, sanitation, and rubbish collection were more likely to improve the residents' health. The community learned a lot about the major health problems and a great deal more about the range of solutions available to them, as well as the realities of costs and available resources within the community to meet these needs.

The issue of participation is also dealt with in Chapter 4, when different research methods are described in detail.

Expectations aroused by research

Traditional 'top-down' research by outsiders tends to raise local people's expectations, and they may expect it to solve long-standing problems. People may assume that basic research will inevitably lead to money being spent locally in a development programme. The different interests of the people involved may create very different expectations of the research findings and the action these may lead to. The best way of preventing unrealistic expectations is, of course, to involve the local group fully in the planning and execution of the research itself, whenever this is practicable.

Not only is a local group likely to get unrealistic expectations from a research project, but the agency staff themselves may fall victims to the same mystique. The pressure to move automatically from research to commitment must be resisted. You should never allow the research to become a prescription for action if this is not fully justified.

> Agricultural programme in western Sudan: The local representatives of two agencies identified possible action related to irrigation and seed banks as a priority for rural development during a short visit to an area in Sudan. They came to these conclusions without serious and systematic research; and this was their first mistake. They then started a base-line survey of the area which assumed that both irrigation and seed banks would be supported. The second mistake was to use this biased survey as the basis for project intervention instead of treating it as the base-line document for beginning to think about a project intervention. Various programmes were then started and technical staff came and went, but much of this activity did not relate to the initial survey, although it was this survey which acted as the justification for the development interventions. After nearly two years a second consultant was hired who was obliged to reformulate the programme completely by referring to the original survey, cross-checking the initial assumptions upon which the programmes were based, as set by the two agencies, and then redesigning the whole programme. The premature pressure for some sort of development intervention led in this case to a lack of correlation between the original consultant's survey reports and the actual implementation of the programme, which was haphazard and did not take into account the information supplied in the reports.

To avoid raising local expectations take care to explain who you are, and what your agency stands for. Always try to make it clear that the research might not lead to action.

Action research in Malawi: An Oxfam-sponsored research

12

exercise in rural Malawi was designed to identify the major problems and priorities of some of the most vulnerable people in a district. It was realised that a major problem would be that the research would raise people's expectations. The researchers were specifically trained to ensure that they made it as clear as possible that they were there to learn from people, not to provide immediate assistance with their problems. The researchers had to practise their explanations in front of colleagues to ensure that they could avoid anything which might raise false expectations. The research team explained to the villagers that the research was intended to assist the government and other agencies to improve development planning in the country and district rather than to provide immediate help for the six villages covered by the research. But in spite of all these precautions, people still hoped the research would lead to immediate benefits. (See also Appendix 6.)

Constraints on conducting research

This section deals with some of the main constraints on research, which is never carried out under perfect conditions; there are always difficulties to be overcome.

Government attitude
The right of an agency to operate in another country depends upon the will of the host country. Permission to do research should normally have been part of a Country Agreement which set out the conditions under which the development agency operates. If for some reason research has been omitted from the agreement, or had conditions attached to it, then negotiations might have to be undertaken with an appropriate Ministry to get permission to do research. If political conditions in the country generally, or in the area you are working in, are good, and your agency has a positive image with the relevant Ministry, research permission should be readily forthcoming. But if the country is riven by bitter internal conflicts, or your agency is operating in a climate of mistrust and suspicion, then a relatively simple research project may present itself to official minds as a major diplomatic issue, and you will need all your patience, tact and

persuasiveness to get the project accepted. Under such difficult conditions, research sometimes simply 'isn't on.'

Alternatively, you may take the view that anything which is not explicitly forbidden by your Country Agreement, and which is covered by your general statement of agency aims, is clearly defensible, and go ahead with your research without seeking official clearance. This strategy might initially save you time and trouble. But be prepared for misunderstandings, and be ready to explain your research in a calm, and diplomatic way if an anxious and ill-informed official — from the police, for example — decides that you are engaged in some kind of spying activity, or something else harmful to the interests of the government. Social researchers are used to having their inquiries misunderstood; and the idea of the spy has diffused all over the world.

It is a better tactic, if you want to make a rapid start and cut through the red tape, to notify your most friendly senior contacts in an appropriate Ministry informally that you wish to do some research on a specific topic — agricultural productivity, or mother-child health issues — in a particular locality, so that in the event of misunderstandings you can say to inquirers, 'Mr X and Mrs Y at the Ministry know what we are doing here, and can tell you about our work.'

In short, government, whether through policy directives or the attitude of particular officials, can often be a significant source of constraints on research. It is inevitable that some of the activities of foreign development agencies, in particular, should arouse a certain amount of misunderstanding and mistrust; and one of the best ways to counter this is by the greatest possible openness. Try to collaborate with sympathetic officials wherever possible.

The style of research can also be a factor: a major formal survey with a large number of interviewers will have a high profile and inevitably attract official attention, whereas a research method such as participant observation, or informal group discussions will normally attract far less attention. Try to be aware of issues or questions most likely to be controversial, or politicised. Ensure that good local contacts are maintained. Try and carry out as much of the research as possible in a low-profile manner.

Conflicts and emergencies

Civil wars, famines, earthquakes and other highly disruptive situations create special problems for research. There is a tendency among those directly involved to produce highly-coloured, partisan accounts of what has been happening and, as has been said many times, in a war the first casualty is the truth.

It is only possible to get a useful account of conditions in a war-zone by patient informal interviewing of refugees, but this will need careful scrutiny and cross-checking to compensate for any elements of exaggeration which may very understandably have crept into the accounts given by traumatised people. Such information may be very important if you need to gauge the extent of food shortages which may be threatening, or the proportions of local populations who have fled from their homes. By careful cross-checking about dates and times at which people left their communities, and asking how many people had not yet left, you can form a picture of the extent of the flight. By use of regional census information, and with the help of sympathetic and knowledgeable local officials, you can build up a picture of the total numbers of people leaving an area, for whom some kind of relief provision may be needed.

In situations of major disruption, relief workers are likely to make serious over-estimates of the scale of disaster if they do not carry out normal cross-checking procedures. In general, the more serious the emergency, the greater the need for cool, thoughtful appraisal of the extent of the threats to people, food, crops, and water supplies. Nothing is gained by taking a few unconfirmed and sketchy reports at face value, and calling for major, costly relief programmes. It is better to take a little more time, research more thoroughly, reduce the margins of error by a variety of cross-checks, and then call for a more realistic level of outside assistance.

The most important information and analysis, however, will not be based on the refugees' immediate experiences at all, but will be concerned with that has been happening and will be happening politically in the zone from which they have fled. The agency will need to understand why they have fled, what caused the underlying problems, and what are the implications in the short, medium, and longer terms. The two basic questions will be, is there a likelihood of their being able to return to their homes at any foreseeable point, and how that likelihood — or the lack of it — will affect the planning of programmes of provision.

In 1982 when 50,000 displaced people from Uganda arrived in neighbouring Rwanda, the Red Cross reported that 20 per cent of children under five were in a state of serious malnutrition. This figure was accepted by UNHCR and by the government, neither of which had reason to doubt the Red Cross findings. The data were transmitted to NGOs, and plans were made for a massive response based on emergency feeding procedures.

An Oxfam doctor managed to reach the camp within a couple of days and pointed out that the 20 per cent figure was unusually high and, if it were true, was an indicator that the whole refugee population was in a very bad way indeed.

Further enquiries revealed that the Red Cross data had been collected at the emergency health post in the camp. In other words, the sample was severely biased because the only children to be taken to the health post were children who were already ill, many of them with intestinal complaints. A random nutritional survey was put into operation and within half a day reliable data were available which put the nutritional status of under-fives at a figure which was normal for southern Uganda at that time of the year. The nutritional status of the whole population was therefore acceptable. Plans for the emergency feeding were scrapped.

This case history illustrates two points: that in an emergency people can accept data uncritically and appear to want to believe in a worst-case situation; that in a crisis, fieldworkers can set aside normal and sound research techniques and in this case it took two days before anyone pointed out that the data were skewed because of the poor sample which was measured.

In situations of social disruption, you must take particular care not to put people at risk by asking them to collect information for you. Information which in peace-time is innocuous, such as the whereabouts of a village, or the number of people resident there, may have alarming implications if there are guerrillas or counter-insurgency forces operating in the area.

16

Cultural factors: gender relations and power structures

In many societies there is a structural inequality which militates against the participation of certain groups in the research process. There is often, to use Freire's term, a 'culture of silence' — a passive resistance to outside intervention which can easily manifest itself in a lack of co-operation with researchers. This lack of co-operation may well be based on bitter past experiences and it might be necessary to identify the origins of the problem before progress can be made and useful research carried out.

Access to certain groups is often restricted, for example, non-local researchers' access to women in some cultures; and the physically or mentally handicapped are likely to be kept hidden from outsiders in their own homes. The silent members of society are often the very people you need to hear from, and include in your work. (See Appendix 5) It is important to identify who these people are and where they are. Such people need to be given the opportunity to express themselves, which means that the researcher needs to develop a style which permits this.

A woman evaluator from India, who was used to working with women in a semi-closed society, was able to achieve in Sudan what she was told would be impossible. She succeeded in holding meetings with large numbers of poor women, and getting them to speak openly about their views on their economic role. Previously the women project staff had accepted the traditional view that women would not and could not meet for such discussions, because inevitably the project staff were themselves a part of that same tradition, despite their professional roles.

For people who do not usually have the opportunity to voice their concerns, research can be very positive and enabling in itself because it can encourage such people to articulate their needs. Sensitive research can help give the voiceless a voice. Participatory research can sometimes lead to actions which break with tradition, and in doing so it may be empowering for groups involved. This in turn may lead to hostile reactions from those losing privilege or power. The researchers need to foresee

17

such tensions, and think carefully about the balance of benefits which will result.

Where access to a group is more than usually difficult, extra time will be needed to develop the appropriate contacts, build trust, and overcome inhibitions at both a group and individual level. The methods used in the research need to take account of cultural differences. It is a matter of judgement how far it is possible or desirable to work against the grain of local customs and perceptions regarding certain gender issues. A group working in Maharashtra divided the health team into a male group and a female group in order to discuss the same issues with separate groups of men and women in the villages where they worked. This proved to be an effective strategy. In a different context, where women might have something to gain by discussions being held jointly with men, a more challenging and innovative strategy might be tried.

In some cultures the whole idea of asking direct questions may be unacceptable or even the height of rudeness. A special approach will be needed to cope with such cultural constraints. (See later section on Asking Questions, p. 53.)

There is no escape from the problem of power in development research, and it has two distinct aspects: the power structure of the society being investigated, and secondly, the subculture of the development agency itself.

The national and local structures you are working with will involve differences of wealth, security, and influence between groups. This will usually be most noticeable in terms of ownership of crucial resources — land, water, animals, vehicles, houses, and businesses. The 'ownership' of government and military jobs may also be crucial. Leaders, chiefs, notables, professionals, or simply people of high rank, or particular ethnic or tribal origins, will be making decisions which fit their own needs and interests, and affect the people you wish to help in all kinds of ways.

You will usually be working to help the people who lack power and influence, and who are subject to the decisions of the power-holders. Many of the problems faced in a local area are made worse by the pervasive differences in political and economic power e.g. the system of land ownership, the low wages paid to day labourers, the use of thugs to intimidate those

18

attempting to organise labourers. You will frequently find that attractive development initiatives will run up against the power structure, or cause friction with it. Local people will be the real experts on how the system of power and influence really works at grassroots level, and therefore which initiatives will be feasible, and which will not.

Any development agency has its own cultural and political values, which are partly external to the local society and partly involved with it, since the agency inevitably becomes a player, if usually a minor one, in the local power structure. An agency tends to recruit as staff people who are often relatively highly trained, and middle-class in the national system. Both expatriates and locals may have a commitment to helping the least advantaged groups, but when viewed by the local poor, all the agency staff may appear as wealthy, powerful and secure, even though in their own eyes they feel none of these things.

It is sometimes argued that middle-class people cannot do effective and sensitive research on the problems faced by the poor because their own backgrounds mean they have not experienced poverty. We reject this argument. Membership of a particular class is at best only a rough-and-ready guide to how people think, and to their moral values. The most important question to ask about a particular researcher regarding their appropriateness and competence to work with poorer people is not, what is their class origin, but what are their human qualities? Do they have empathy? Are they sensitive to the needs of others? Do they have the imagination to grasp what life is like when, for example, all fuelwood and drinking water have to be carried for half a day by the family who uses them? Above all, good researchers have to be good listeners, and be willing to control their own egos sufficiently to grasp what other people can tell them, and draw appropriate conclusions. These skills are not confined to any particular class or subculture.

Resources
Time, money, and energy will all be consumed in a research project. For any research you need to ask if staff can be spared and if money will be available and energy forthcoming, and you need to ask if the community being investigated can be called on to assist, at the particular time envisaged. This requires

19

detailed knowledge of the seasonal patterns of community work. In agricultural communities, the two busiest times of the year are the planting and harvesting seasons, and it is a safe assumption that no-one in such a community will have any time for you during these seasons. It is far better to plan your research for one of the slack periods of the year, and community members will be able to tell you when this is; and, as we shall argue later, you need to study a community at several points in the productive year, to avoid distortions of various kinds.

There are a wide range of different methods available to assist in the collection of information. Some of these are very simple and inexpensive, whilst others entail complex planning and some statistical knowledge and can be very expensive and time-consuming. In the choice of an appropriate method it will be important to take account of the needs, the expense, and the time available before deciding. The large-scale sample survey, where hundreds of people need to be contacted and inter-viewed, is one of the slowest and most energy-costly methods available, not only because of the data collection phase, but also because the analysis of the data contained in several hundred questionnaires may take months rather than weeks. Supposing the essential information could have been obtained for one-tenth of the cost, and in a quarter of the time — what 'price' the com-prehensiveness and rigour of the survey? It would not be sensi-ble to spend £2,000 on researching a project which will distrib-ute another £5,000-worth of help to 25 people. But on the other hand, if very large sums of money might be committed to a pro-ject, the extra time and money needed for a well-designed sur-vey might well justify themselves. It might be better to spend £5,000 on a survey and learn that it would be unwise to commit £100,000, than to 'save' the initial £5,000, carry out more impres-sionistic research, get the wrong answers, and then see £100,000 wasted on a failing project.

So, to summarise the resources issue: the more the project will cost, and the greater the impact it will have on other people, the more ready you should be to spend what is needed by way of feasibility research. If in doubt, keep the research costs to below 10 per cent of the projected project costs.

2 STRATEGIC ISSUES IN PLANNING SOUND RESEARCH

Suppose you have decided that research is needed, and some issues have been clarified with the help of local people. Before committing yourself to one or several of the possible methods to be discussed in Chapter 3, there are some preliminary matters to be decided, each of which will have a bearing on what you do and how you do it. These involve deciding whom to focus on, your 'unit of analysis'; thinking about when and for how long your research will be conducted, and the implications of the time limits; controlling for bias and making the research properly representative; avoiding certain common pitfalls; choosing the researchers; and styles of research.

The unit of analysis

There are two distinct issues to be considered. The first issue is easy: it involves having a clear sense of where the study begins and ends, the cut-off points. This is largely a matter of being certain that you are studying the five villages on the east side of the mountain, but not the ones on the north, south and west sides. Or that you are concerned with children from one to five. Or disabled persons, defined by some specific criterion of disability. This is because research must end somewhere, and if you are not careful, local pressures may make your research net expand to cover ever larger populations, because of the 'arousal of expectations' issue mentioned in the preceding section.

The second issue is more difficult: it involves the strategic level at which you will study the research question — individual, household, community, or institutions. The decision to make a particular unit of analysis the focus of the research is all-important. The research questions very often point directly to specific units: if you are concerned with mother-and-child health, then mothers will obviously be primary informants, and so indeed might children. But mothers are not all identical. First-time mothers may have a different set of problems from mothers who have had several children; and grandmothers may have different views on child care from their own daughters, themselves now mothers but who have been exposed to more schooling. The health-care workers who will be dealing with the mothers and children will also have information, and may be divided by age, specialisation or experience. So, although 'mothers' will have to be key figures in your study, they will need to be separated into several types of mothers, and the health-care workers will also need to be interviewed.

The household is far from being a straightforward unit of analysis. In the past, researchers were happy to talk about 'the household' as if it were a unit which pooled its members' interests, and met their needs in a fair-minded way. But recent research shows this assumption is often questionable, for two different kinds of reasons. First, households come in many different forms, composed of a variety of persons in all kinds of roles. Some households may contain an unmarried brother and sister of advanced years. Some households may have two generations, and three married couples. Some households may be a man, and his wife, and one widowed parent of either husband or wife. Many households consisting of a woman and her children may be headed up by the woman for 10 months of the year, while her husband — if she still has one — is away working as a migrant labourer. So it is unwise to assume any particular composition to 'the household', and any particular profile of producers and consumers. Some households have land but not enough adult labour; some households have labour, but no land. Some households have few producers but many consumers.

Another major reason for not assuming too much about the household in a research setting is to do with gender relations. The income enjoyed by a household may sometimes be distributed between all members on the basis of need, but quite often there are cultural rules or expectations about who gets what. In some cultures, men get first choice of the available food, and women and children eat later from what is left. In such cases, men need not be consciously aware that they are taking at the expense of the rest of the household; or the custom may be rationalised by men and women as essential because men are culturally defined as warriors, or farmers 'doing the heaviest work'. A man may feel that cash earned by him through crop sales or paid labour is his to keep, consume, or give out to his wife as he sees fit. An increase in his income may not be shared with his wife and children. He might decide to buy a bicycle with it, to reduce his travel time when going to work. A woman may have earnings she is unwilling to give to her husband, because she uses the money to feed and clothe her children, or pay for their schooling. The researcher cannot, therefore, assume, that sums of money which reach one member of the household will necessarily be shared with others. A benefit targeted at mothers-and-children should be paid directly to the mother.

It is a commonplace finding that, although households may benefit from irrigated agricultural schemes, in that their cash incomes are higher than before they joined the scheme, there may at the same time be a decline in the nutritional status of their children. This is for a complex of reasons: such as less food being grown by the family, the range of locally available foods for purchase becoming smaller, and the women having less time to prepare food. Yet, from the perspective of national economic planners, such a 'household' has now become 'better off'.

. The identification of the poorest categories, households, or individuals presents particular problems for research, and these will be discussed again in later sections. First, simple visibility: are the poor people in the research locality physically present when the researchers are active, or are they away, as labour migrants, or spending their days and nights far from where the research team are, watching over browsing animals, or gathering natural resources in marginal areas? Secondly, the poorest are often forgotten by their more fortunate neighbours, so relatively casual inquiries may not identify them. Thirdly, people who think a research group may be willing to help them, may describe themselves as the poorest, although there are others poorer than they are. Various methods can be used to overcome these difficulties, and we discuss these under Rapid Rural Appraisal, (p. 66) and the use of indicators (p. 78). At this point, we will simply note that mapping a community, dwelling by dwelling, and finding out the names of all the people who live in each dwelling is a way of making sure people are not overlooked, and this can be followed up with a wealth-ranking exercise. Both the mapping and the ranking work can usually best be done with help from local people. (See also Participatory Rural Appraisal, p. 74.)

To take a different kind of example: suppose representatives of a remote community were seeking a loan to buy a vehicle which would allow the members of the community to visit a market town, for economic and health reasons. It might be important to know who visits the market town, how often, for what purposes; and how people think this pattern might change if there were a vehicle making the journey once a week. Then, too, it might be important to know how often people would use the vehicle at specific prices for the journey.

There are all kinds of possible pitfalls in this apparently simple set of issues. If we assume too quickly that the unit of analysis must self-evidently be adult villagers as individuals we may miss the importance of the fact that the individuals usually live in families and households, and that their travel decisions might be altered by whether or not another member of their household is willing or able to make the journey on the same day. In practice, to cut down on expenses, it would be probable that members of the same households, or even of closely-related people living in separate households, would 'run errands' for each other. So a questionnaire based solely on a village of 300 adults, treating them all as discrete individuals, would run the risk of seriously overestimating the numbers of paying passengers the vehicle might attract, and thus put the economics of its operation on shaky foundations. Yet, on the other hand, to assume that there should be a single questionnaire answered by a representative of each household would risk losing sight of gender distinctions. A man might see himself as the person likely to use the vehicle, and think of his wife as staying at home. The wife, for her part, might have definite reasons for wanting to make her own journeys independently, particularly if the market town has a health clinic and she has children.

There could be various solutions to such a problem. One course of action would be to ask half the village as individuals (half male, half female) and the other half as households (asking the most active man and woman in each household, but interviewing them separately), and compare the differences in responses and estimates, if any. A second solution would be to interview individuals, but to include a question to everyone on the lines of 'Would you still be likely to make this journey once a week (month, quarter...) if another member of your household were already going?' There could then be a comparison of the pattern of answers between men and women informants.

But there is one serious problem about all these approaches, and that is that, because they are a study of future activity, they rely on statements of intentions by asking hypothetical questions, such as 'How often would you be likely to visit the market town?'. Experienced researchers try to avoid the use of predictions and hypothetical questions (ones which use the word 'would'). Sometimes such questions are unavoidable, but they need to be used with caution, and you should not rely solely on answers to them for your information, but always try and cross-check.

One way out of this dilemma would be to supplement the study of the particular community with a 'control study' of a neighbouring community, as similar as possible in its social composition in terms of numbers of farmers, artisans, and landless people, which already possessed a mini-bus service. The data on actual observed usage would probably be a better guide than hypothetical statements of intent. The researcher should, ideally, travel on the vehicle a number of times, noting who was travelling and asking them for the reasons for their journey. (We deliberately put 'reasons' in the plural, because people very often have several compatible reasons for doing something, and a good question should never assume there is only one.)

Moving to larger units, such as a whole community, a co-operative or a cluster of neighbouring villages, brings new decisions about units of data collection and subsequent analysis. If you are dealing with a population of farmers, for example, then class, here understood as the size of land-holding, will be of significance, and you might wish to think about the different constraints which affect the landless, small, medium, and larger farmers. Your unit of analysis will need to take these differences into account.

In a study of the needs of rural people in Botswana for fuel-wood, an area was chosen in which wood around the village had been used up. One of the objects of inquiry was to find out how people obtained fuelwood, and who was most likely to buy it.

The results were surprising. If the researchers had relied on a few casual conversations with some of the more prominent members of the community, they might have heard the views of the richer farmers only. These people own tractors, and they never purchase wood on the market. Instead, once every few months, they send one of their sons off with a tractor, who drives a long distance and hauls back a large supply. Families without tractors tend to gather wood more frequently, and from closer at hand. The poorer families have to send someone to forage for wood every 24 hours. But the category most likely to purchase wood turned out to be labour-poor families, who simply could not spare anyone from the most pressing food-producing and income-generating activities, and in particular, old women living alone. They could not make the long journeys needed, and had no-one to send. If they did not buy wood, they could not cook their food.

In this study the unit of analysis was firstly, the household but secondly, households reclassified by income and by amount of labour power. A small selection of households, not subdivided in this way, might have missed either the rich or the very poor, and in each case their actual behaviour went rather against the grain of common-sense expectations, which would be that the rich were most likely to buy fuelwood, and the poor, least likely.

Choosing the right unit of analysis is crucial to the success of any research exercise, and it must be defined at an early stage of the research. You may decide that you need to carry out a special pre-research exercise, a 'pilot study', to establish the best unit of analysis for your purposes.

Questions of time

An obvious limitation on any data-collection effort is the time available in which to carry out the work. The first question to answer therefore is **how much time have you got?** It will often be less than you would like. The time available may be limited by the contracting agency, which needs information in a hurry to enable it to continue with its programme, or other constraints such as access, weather, and, of course, money; so the next important question is **how much research and research time can you afford?** The answer to this question is also likely to be pragmatic and have more to do with the priority other people (funders, government officials, senior managers) put on your research. The resources at your disposal are unlikely to be adequate for the job in hand; but this is the reality for fieldworkers the world over, and what distinguishes them from people carrying out individually-determined academic research.

Another time-related question is at what point research should be done. Experience has shown that it is never too late to start a research programme, even in a project that is already functioning. Existing staff can be re-trained and directed towards a more thoughtful collection of information, monitoring, and reassessment of their activities. If it is never too late to start research, it is also much better to start early. Relief and development programmes may begin in a hurry, especially in an emergency, and if adequate information is not collected, misunderstandings may develop.

In southern Sudan an emergency water programme for refugees was started on the assumption that the need was for three months only. After nearly two years the programme was evaluated, and the evaluation report highlighted many important points that had previously never been understood, such as local beliefs regarding the siting of water sources, and revealed a much higher participation by local people, as opposed to refugees, in the water programme than had been originally envisaged. The moral of the story is that, although the initial intervention was to meet emergency demands, the process of research and investigation should have started with the start of the water programme, which might then have operated more effectively.

Some research entails a close look at seasonal changes. A survey carried out at one point in the year will miss a great deal which is of importance. Data collected shortly after a harvest will be very different from data collected after a period of shortage, particularly regarding nutritional status, disposable income or assets, and social relations. So research will have to be planned to report on at least two seasons in a year if it is to be reliable and comprehensive.

Migrations of labourers, nomads, and others may be seasonal, which means that it is only too easy for interviewers to arrive in a community and be unaware that many people are missing who are working elsewhere at that time of year. A static survey which does not take production and residence differences over time into account is of limited value. But it is not necessary for the research to be spun out over a full calendar year, since local informants will always have a very lively and clear perception of the major changes which occur cyclically. It will help the researchers to understand these changes if they sit down with the local people and work out the year's cycle, and note what happens during each month, the local names for the different seasons and the climatic and residential changes which occur.

The research timetable

Time is required to establish trust and to build up a fuller knowledge of a community. If you are interested in attitudes it is of particular importance to allow ample time for relationships to develop to the extent that attitudes can emerge and local people allow the researchers a sufficiently accurate and intimate knowledge of the community, rather than a 'public relations' image of the community as problem-free.

When you are working with certain types of group you will need to allow more time for the research programme; it may take longer to recruit and train research assistants, to win a group's trust and gain access to its members. Language may create problems: the secondary materials may be more difficult to locate.

Many researchers underestimate the 'set-up time' needed for preparation, training assistants, and obtaining research permission; they then find that at the end of the exercise they have run out of time to do the all-important analysis, so are obliged to write a report full of undigested material, of little use to anyone. It might well take a couple of months to draw up job descriptions, advertise, recruit and have people ready to start work. It will then take a couple of weeks to train them in the approach and methods being used.

It is possible to estimate the time required for some procedures with a little more certainty. For example, suppose you find out by running a pilot, or trial, that a straightforward questionnaire or survey takes half an hour; if you require a survey of 2,000 people to be carried out within ten days, you can calculate that you will need 33 fieldworkers to cover the 2,000 people selected as a sample, assuming that each fieldworker manages six interviews a day, and works ten days in succession without an official rest day. (33 interviewers x 6 interviews per day x 10 days = 198. The remaining 20 interviews can be done by the research supervisor as one of a number of 'quality checks'.) If it is easy to find interview subjects because they are in large, compact communities, and ready to co-operate, then the estimate of six interviews per day might be raised to eight or nine, and the number of interviewers reduced accordingly. If surveys are being carried out at village level it should be possible to estimate the time required for one village, and then multiply this by the number of villages to be covered. You then need to assess how accessible people are likely to be and when they will be available for interviews. It is important not just to include the most easily accessible people, those at home during daylight hours or who live closer to the centre of the village. So you must calculate the time required to get to the houses further from the village centre, and to meet a cross-section of the community. Remember that men and women are likely to be free or available at different times of the day or in different places. Having made your estimates of the time your survey will take, it is probably wise to add some extra time, in case things do not go quite as smoothly as you expect.

The interviewer is not the only person whose time is valuable: the people being interviewed also value their time. You should be aware of the opportunity cost to those being interviewed — what would they have been doing if they weren't answering your questions? Try to ensure that you ask for the minimum time possible from your respondents compatible with obtaining the information required.

Try to assess which stages of the research process could be

speeded up: could the writing be done faster? Is time being wasted by using unnecessarily long questionnaires?

When selecting staff, make sure that appropriate staff are chosen for the different stages of the work: designing and planning, the actual data collection, and the analysis of results. Some staff will be quick thinking, and keen to be involved in more direct action; others are more suited to a slower, sensitive listening role; others will be better at the report writing, and so on.

Continuous research or a snapshot?

A key question which will relate to the time required or available for research is whether the research will take place over a period of time through a prolonged process of data collection or be a one-off exercise. A continuous research process may occur as part of normal monitoring, or a series of follow-up surveys, regular updating of data through new samples, or result from stringing together a series of 'snapshots' over a period of time. The one-off or snapshot exercise will give an image of reality and define certain social facts at a given point in time. Both approaches have advantages, and sometimes only a one-off exercise may be feasible due to a lack of pre-existing data, the need to make short-term decisions, or the lack of resources for continuous research.

The danger of taking a snapshot view of a group is that it can often be extremely misleading or indicate a state which is normal to that group but is interpreted by outsiders as abnormal. For example, many so-called emergencies are identified as such by outsiders, when in fact the nutritional status of the group may always be comparatively poor. Thus, longer-term solutions rather than a short-term 'emergency' intervention are necessary if the situation is to be changed for the better. The snapshot view often does little to help analyse causes, although it can identify symptoms of longer-term problems. Thus, while it helps to identify which group is destitute and how many people are in the group, it may not assist in understanding why they are destitute, for how long they have been in this state, and how long they might remain destitute if no intervention were made by the development agency.

Continuous research allows comparison over time and should give a more accurate picture of changes and what is normal for a given group. For example, nutritional data collected only once, which cannot be compared to other information, are not very helpful in indicating whether the group's nutritional status is improving, static or deteriorating, and whether the present nutritional status is normal, abnormal, or reflects a seasonal bias. A project should possess base-line data for the area or group with which it is working — that is, descriptive data about the position at a particular point in time, from which changes can be plotted. It would then be possible to compare new information showing social, economic and other changes, with the base-line information and other follow-up information. The textbooks all say that any programme must start with a base-line survey, and this would certainly be desirable; but, in practice, data collection often comes at a time when programmes are already functioning, as a part of the normal monitoring process. Although a traditional base-line survey may not exist, if the material collected during a project cycle is consistent, in that similar information is collected in similar ways, then at least this will provide for the possibility of making comparisons over time and will enable decisions to be made as to changes in the target group and the functioning of the programme.

In addition to making comparisons over time, it is sometimes possible to compare over 'space', by looking at information from similar units. For example, one could compare literacy levels in two villages, the first having joined a development programme ten years previously, the second only recently. It might be found that the level of literacy in the second village is similar to that encountered in the first village at the time it first joined the programme ten years ago. If the village with a well-established programme now demonstrates much lower rates of illiteracy, it is possible to make meaningful and positive comparisons to the village which remained outside the scheme. Using such a method, villages newly entering the programme act as 'control groups' against which to measure the progress of other villages in the scheme.

The processes of monitoring and ongoing research activities should allow for an assessment of change over time. Included in this monitoring should be an attempt to assess what the impact of the programme really is, and separate this from other factors both internal and external to the community. For example, an

31

evaluation of a programme designed to strengthen the food security of a nomadic group should try to assess the impact of the programme on the overall food availability, but will also need to take into account internal factors, such as the decision by more families to enter settled agriculture, and external factors, such as the supply of food aid by other agencies or government control of grain prices in the area.

A balance can sometimes be found between continuous and snapshot approaches to information gathering. Certain types of information will lend themselves to a snapshot approach, but these snapshots can then be incorporated into a longer-term view. For example, a technical survey of the physical availability of water in an area could be carried out and used in a longer-term survey of changing water use in the same area.

Objectivity, subjectivity, and the control of bias

All thoughtful research seeks to control for the biases of both researchers and informants, and a great deal of the advice given in this book is concerned with this issue in one way or another. But professional researchers disagree about just how far in theory or practice it is possible to give an 'objective' account of what is going on between groups of human beings. For some, such as economists, economic historians, experimental psychologists, it should in principle be possible to describe and analyse what human beings do in such a way that errors of fact are eliminated, so that a panel of independent observers would agree that they had seen a man bite a dog, a motorist knock down a pedestrian, a policeman take a bribe, or any one of millions of possible events.

But other researchers, particularly anthropologists, social historians, and sociologists interested in religious or political movements, tend to be sceptical about the reliability and validity of the 'objective' accounts just discussed. They point to the difficulties often experienced by the judges and juries in a court of law in deciding what happened in a legal case, to various philosophical and perceptual problems to do with how far two individuals ever really share experiences of the same 'real world' and to what extent anyone can succeed in communicating such experiences to another person. The headache which apparently incapacitates one person might be shrugged off by another; and a downwardly mobile person might experience as real deprivation conditions which to an upwardly mobile person appear almost luxurious. Consider the loading on the phrases 'slum'; 'shantytown'; 'informal low-income accommodation'; 'squatter settlements'; 'our home'. All are phrases being used to classify the same physical structures, which are objectively present for description. But each classification bears its own weight of subjective values.

Let us return for a moment to the observers who believed they saw a policeman take a bribe. If they saw a policeman stop a motorist, and they saw that the motorist handed over a sum of money before driving away, they might feel sure that what they had seen was a bribe being offered and accepted. They might have overheard the policeman say to the motorist 'I want a contribution from you before I let you go!' and this would have only confirmed them in their conclusions. And 99 times out of 100, their conclusion would have been valid.

But supposing that the motorist is also a policeman, but not in uniform, and that he is in fact being asked for his subscription to the annual police dinner, then the whole event takes on a completely different meaning. The observed events really happened, but their wider context, their true significance, was unknown to the observers, and they reached a false conclusion.

In the case of the 'bribe', the final piece of evidence which would have helped decide the matter would have been the policeman's intentions — if he agreed to give an honest account of them. In this kind of case, we could be clear about his intentions, and there would be a lot of supporting evidence to consider. But even if people are co-operating with researchers, and telling the truth as they see it, it is not always the case that they are clear about their intentions.

Imagine three boys playing truant from school. They are clear about not wanting to be bored in the classroom, but they do not know how their day will end up, or what their specific intentions are, apart from 'having fun'. Sometimes the participants in a political or religious movement are protesting about something — they know what they do not want — but are not at all clear about the future, or their own intentions. At this point, the researchers who seek 'objective knowledge' would be in some difficulties, but those who see their task as the interpretation of the actor's meanings might be able to offer a provisional attempt at understanding what the movement seeks to achieve.

The debate between those who are more optimistic about the possibility of objective research, and those who are more sceptical, will never be resolved, and we do not intend to take sides here. In principle, all researchers should try to be as objective as possible in the way they carry out the research, that is, they should seek for precision and accuracy, and to control bias. But if they are wise, they will never suppose that they have completely succeeded, and they will remain open, right down to the last stages of their research, to the possibility of their having made interpretive errors of all kinds.

But the critics of objectivity are not therefore free to say, 'Since real objectivity is impossible, and since I have a committed political view, I am free to conduct my research in any way I choose, and I shall choose a way which directly furthers my ethical and political values.' They must be just as committed to accuracy, precision, and the control of bias as the seekers after objective reporting. The difference is, they may allow themselves to be more aware of different and conflicting interpretations of the social world, and prefer interpretations of research data which present the findings as tentative, and provisional, rather than conclusive, and written in stone.

Representative results

Good research seeks to give a representative account of the group of people studied, such that all their views are represented, and not merely those views which the researchers approve of or to which they are politically sympathetic. This is for two distinct reasons. Firstly, it is never good research practice to take short-cuts, or to leave views out because you think you know what they are likely to be and so wish to discount them politically. Secondly, it is necessary to represent all views in a community because the success or failure of a development project may depend crucially on the attitudes and interests of people who are not the target beneficiaries of the project. If large land-lords are employers of casual labour, and your project is designed to help landless labourers, the landlords' interests may need to be understood before any scheme to increase the income of the labourers can succeed. This does not mean that the landlords will be given any kind of veto over the project design, but it does mean the researchers need to hear from the landlords, just as clearly as they hear from the labourers.

There is no easy way for either identifying or eradicating bias, in interviewer or interviewee. It is up to each researcher to think about the similarities and differences between himself, or herself and the people with whose lives the research is concerned, and to attempt to become sensitive to how far social differences promote different interpretations about what is going on.

Take time to think about such basic conflicts of interest, perception and reality-definition as are likely to arise between land-lords and tenants (issues of fair rents, and good amenities), between pedestrians and car-drivers (issues about taking the other's speed and needs into account), between employers and employees (wages, quality of work, working conditions), teachers and students (time and quality of teaching), doctors and patients (time, and the wish to get better). In all these pairs of roles, there are possibilities of conflicting definitions of what has been transacted, but there is also the possibility that a careful observer could give a description and analysis of the transactions which would satisfy both sides as being accurate, and un-biased.

One important source of bias involves gender, where men may be blind to the interests, preoccupations, and working lives of women. To begin to come to grips with this issue involves conscious awareness of the need to have women fully involved from the first inception of the research project. By 'fully involved' we mean that women are equal partners in policy making, research design, and all the other phases of the research. Superficial and *ad hoc* consultation is not enough. (See Appendix 5.)

Other sources of bias arise through cultural differences between researchers and informants, which may cluster around issues of rank, age, social origins, skills, religious differences — indeed, an open-ended set of possible issues.

Some pitfalls to be avoided

In an earlier section we argued that it is best to treat the household as a neutral and unknown unit rather than to assume in advance that you know how its members will behave towards each other in matters of economics and domestic budgeting. Similar care is needed with some other loaded terms — class, solidarity, and community.

Avoid false certainty about people's class: Another kind of naive assumption involves the labels given to particular classes. For example, in Latin America people often talk about the 'popular classes', which may be a convenient short-hand description but is extremely difficult to define accurately, because it is not based on any set of agreed, objective criteria. It would not be possible to decide who is a member of the popular classes by measuring income or property rights, for example. It would, however, be possible to ask people whether or not they considered that they were a member of the popular classes. The results would be interesting but totally subjective, in that you would find a range of people who might consider themselves members of such a class irrespective of their actual economic status. It is a label which many people are inclined to attach to themselves, but to withhold from those of whom they disapprove.

Do not assume solidarity: To take another example: you might decide you want to investigate the income levels of female-headed households. It would not be wise to assume that there is any set of common interests shared by such women in a community simply because they share a common sociological characteristic. It is possible that the women in question might not even know of other women who are also household heads, or you might discover marked differences in their income-levels and economic interests. To sum up: to share a common characteristic is no guarantee of a sense of having 'something in common', nor of solidarity, nor common purposes; and you should not make such an assumption in planning research. Indeed, this is precisely the sort of issue which research might help to clarify: if the research suggests a sense of solidarity among women household heads, then something useful might be built upon this bond. But if the solidarity is assumed in some way in the research design, when it is not in fact present, a project may founder on its absence.

Do not assume community: Development workers would often like a physical community — a village, a township — to meet their expectations that it is a natural unit of social co-operation. We see a cluster of dwellings, and allow a romantic fantasy that the physical clustering implies a convergence of interests. All too often small-scale communities turn out to be full of groups with conflicting interests, and histories of competition and even hostility between families and individuals. This does not mean that they are unable to co-operate over the administration of some public good, such as a clinic, a well, or warehouse; but it should signal the dangers of assuming that simply living near to each other automatically leads to something called 'community spirit'. Such an assumption may well lead to problems if certain common interests and characteristics are projected on to a community before there is any real evidence that they exist.

If research seeks to target a group, it is even more important that the different levels of group and individual interests are understood; and that the linkages between them are identified. To take a simple example: in some cultures brothers (married or unmarried) find it easy to co-operate in economic matters, and in others they find it so difficult that nothing positive necessarily follows from two men being brothers. In another culture, men may be part of a clan of several hundred members or more, and may recognise obligations to fellow clansmen, while finding it difficult to trust men from other clans. In times of civil war and famine, the 'unit of trust' tends to shrink, and men will fight for resources against those they co-operated with in better times. The assumptions about the nature of the target group and how the group is being defined need to be made clear and explicit in the research brief and subsequent reports. A system of validation may be required to cross-check that false assumptions have not been made about a group's identity. There are many constraints operating to hide or confuse the perceptions of all actors in this process; in certain countries, governments may claim to represent all views and to have organised people into interest groups.

Do not read rural patterns into urban contexts: One major failing of development planners and researchers alike is that they are tempted to transfer rural models to urban contexts. Some development workers base their experience and ideas on rural work and arrive in urban areas with preconceptions about the degree to which ideas of community and family operate. In a rural context, a neighbour may be someone who will exchange help over agricultural task, because both households have small land-holdings and face common problems. But in an urban context, it is much less likely that two neighbours are involved in the same kind of economic activity, and there may be nothing which predisposes them to help each other. However, schemes for small loans, which require high rates of repayment to remain viable, sometimes work better in urban shanty towns than in rural communities, because the money economy may be unfamiliar to a land-based society, and has not become part of the system of moral evaluations.

Avoid over-reliance on particular informants: Strictly speaking,anyone who gives you information can be thought of as an 'informant'. But this section is about a special problem: many researchers use people they think of as 'key informants' for much of their information about the community they are researching, because these are people who have shown willingness to help them from early on in their first contacts with the community, and seem confident, knowledgeable, and articulate.

Inevitably, most key informants will have their own biases and their own perspectives, based on their social standing in the community, and any information from them needs to be cross-checked or validated against the views of other people. Some development workers are strongly critical of any reliance upon key informants because they believe that this can provide researchers with an excuse to avoid talking directly to a wider range of people. It has even been argued that many of the failures of development planning can be traced to the ill-considered but widespread use of such informants. It is true that some academic studies have relied on information from a single informant, when, for example, a life-history is elicited at length and published by itself. But such a single focus will not do for a development programme where money is to be spent for wider purposes.

Some of the risks of using key informants are evident; if they are all men, or all women, the views of the other sex may go unheard. If they are all senior people, then the often sharply differing views of their juniors may go unconsidered. Secondly, there is a tendency for certain people to become 'professional informants', people who make a speciality of talking authoritatively to outsiders. They may well feel they know all the answers before you have started asking the questions, because they have already worked for every student, aid agency, and survey team for the past ten years and are certain they know what you really need to know! If your informant is also your interpreter you are even more likely to be given a heavily edited version of what is being said: what the interpreter thinks you need to know instead of an accurate translation. Interpreters need to be carefully trained to stop them abbreviating, and 'cleaning up' what is said by an interviewee. In addition, the professional informant may often not be from the community itself but someone marginal to it, from a different tribe, ethnic group or caste, so may not in fact be well integrated. In conclusion, be wary of key informants; only use them when you can cross-check what they are telling you, and try to be aware of their personal biases.

The informant should be appropriate to the information you are seeking. A male government official posted from another area is likely to be a good source of information on those things which affect his job but is unlikely to know much about child-rearing; whereas the local traditional birth attendant will know about childbirth and women's health, but less about how government officials check the co-operative's accounts.

Choosing the researchers

The principal questions are to what extent and in what ways can local people most usefully participate in the research, and how far will experienced or expert researchers be needed? Let us assume that a research problem has been identified, with the helpof the local people or on their initiative. There are three conventional phases to research: design, data collection, and analysis. Each stage may require slightly different sorts of people to carry it out.

For research design it may be advisable to get some initial expert guidance, whether this means consulting a handbook, having a discussion with an academic or specialised civil servant, or writing for advice to an individual or organisation. If the research is properly designed, it may then be possible to carry out most or all of it using local people, who may be willing to participate because they see themselves as having a strong interest in the outcome.

Research on the effects of structural adjustment: In one African country it was felt that NGOs should monitor the effects of an IMF adjustment plan on public services and the lives of poor people. Unfortunately, the instigators of the research started with an assumption of what the conclusions would be (i.e. that the plan would be detrimental), and then sought to find a way of proving it. They were probably right in their assumption, but it clouded discussions of the methodology because they were seeking to provide the proof rather than to provide information from which conclusions could be drawn. Secondly, clear terms of reference based on advice from professional researchers were not produced at an early stage. Thirdly, it was not recognised that to obtain statistically significant results very large-scale surveys would be required. Alternatively, shorter, more impressionistic studies would require a standardised format and need to be carried out over a period of years. They would have to include comparative material collected before the effects of the adjustment plan were being felt.

The failure to seek professional advice on the research at the outset and to appreciate the likely scale of the research required for such monitoring led to several false starts and lost opportunities. Nearly five years passed with little useful information being produced and the chance for monitoring was lost.

In data collection, it is important that the people collecting the information understand the research design, and that, if not themselves drawn from the local group, they are acceptable to them. The local community may be able to supply people to help, particularly secondary school pupils, teachers, and others.

Such people may need to be properly paid even though the project is for the long-term benefit of their community. Never assume that significant free time can or should be given, especially during busy periods. The issue should be sensitively explored and negotiated, without preconceptions on the agency's side.

Local participation and experts

Data collection may need expertise if, for example, it is necessary to carry out testing of blood or water samples. This expertise should be obtained within the region whenever possible.

In a drought-recovery programme supported by Oxfam, a research project was undertaken to monitor and analyse the changes in nutritional levels of the population, and the recovery of vegetation and livestock after a drought. Existing food-aid monitors were integrated into the research programme, through their collecting information on the communities they visited. The data these teams collected was collated and compared with other data collected from aerial surveys, drought and rainfall monitoring stations. The findings were then discussed in a series of seminars prior to publishing the results of a computer-assisted analysis carried out by professional researchers.

. There may be a need for specific expert skills if computer processing or laboratory analysis are required. During the analysis stage there may be an opportunity to test out some of the apparent causal links with the local community. If, for example, the researchers were trying to find out why attendance at health clinics was low, then the suggested reasons thrown up by the data-collection phase could be further validated by being referred back to local people, to check on their plausibility.

If you decide to employ professional staff for some phase of your research, make sure that the people concerned have a proven track record in research in less-developed countries, or have carried out research on behalf of agencies with appropriate priorities. Sometimes, experts 'travel badly' and cannot improvise or adjust to a field situation, and to the need to consult ordinary rural people. The professional should be willing to explain the research method being used and why that method is the method of choice, necessary for the needs of the research. Any reluctance to explain, or failure to explain in a clear and understandable way, is a bad sign.

Such professionals will expect specific and explicit information from you, with clearly written 'terms of reference' comprehensively detailing what is required of the research. Disappointment with the results of research can often be traced to confused and mixed messages from the commissioning agency and lack of clarity in the brief provided for the research team.

Various factors will be important in choosing staff to carry out the research. These may include their ethnic background, gender, languages, level of education, and experience. Before recruiting it is important to prioritise these factors in terms of the jobs to be done. Thus you might decide that it is essential that at least one interviewer is a Spanish-speaking woman, and then hire accordingly.

It is always important to consider the impact of using different kinds of people as researchers. For example, in many societies it is almost impossible for a man to interview women effectively, or for women to interview men. Social origins may also be a sensitive matter: a local researcher with a high status may be seen as intimidating by low-status informants. Seniority may be an additional complication: if your field researchers are young secondary school pupils, because they are literate and have breaks from the school programme which make them available, they may nevertheless need special instruction in how to talk sufficiently respectfully to older men and women who are not educated.

In certain societies it may be useful to use 'cultural brokers', people of mixed descent who cut across normal cultural/ethnic lines and therefore may have better access than usual to the whole group. In one research programme a tribal woman was employed who spoke a tribal language but had been taken away from her community whilst young and had worked as a maid in different countries, where she learned both Spanish and English. On her return to her community she was able to communicate with government officials in Spanish, American aid workers in English, and with her community in her mother tongue. She was also more confident than other women in the community and had no problems talking to or interpreting for men.

Training the field team

It is often possible for research to be carried out using a high proportion of local people after they have been given some basic training. If a survey is being conducted, then the prospective field staff can perform role-playing exercises, with one person acting as questioner and the other as questioned, in front of the trainer and the rest of the group, to get them familiar with introducing themselves, explaining the survey, and taking their respondents gently through the questions, thanking them for their participation, and informing them about how they can keep in touch with the research and its outcomes. If oral history information is needed about some highly specific issue, such as changes in local cropping patterns and crop rotations over a lengthy period, then a 'demonstration' interview can be carried out by the trainer, and helpers can each be asked to select five neighbours from the right age-group, interview them, and report their findings back to a person responsible for writing up the results. It would not be necessary for the helpers themselves to be literate, because they will usually have far better memories than literate people who rely on note-taking, and will have no trouble recalling a set of specific responses on specific issues.

If the research involves tasks where amounts consumed need to be quantified — household woodfuel consumption, for example — then the use of a suitably strong spring balance to weigh wood-loads can be demonstrated, and the training can include taking the group through a typical day, with an emphasis on how, when and where the relevant observations and weighings will need to be made.

Training a field team for survey, interview or observational work requires all the steps in the research procedure to be made explicit, the reasoning behind each step explained, and an account of how the information will contribute to the over-all research task. If a questionnaire is to be used, then the trainer should take the team through it slowly, question by question, discussing the wording of each question, the sorts of answers to be expected, and the ways in which the answers should be written down. Examples of good and bad data recording should be compared. The best practice is to involve the trainees in the very earliest stages of formulating the questionnaire, and testing or 'piloting' it with a few respondents, before committing the team to the final wording. In this way, any problems can be readily identified and corrected: questions which do not produce the intended responses will need to be scrapped, and re-phrased. In any research involving observations and data recording, the team will need to have untypical or problematic patterns and responses discussed.

We cannot leave this topic without again stressing one of our main contentions — the need for a sensitive awareness of gender issues. There are crucial questions which must always be asked about any research: are women involved in identification of research needs? Are they involved in the control of the research? Are they involved in the data collection, processing, and use of the material?

Sometimes, the choice of men or women for a field task will have some important practical issues which revolve around gender differences.

In a survey of woodfuel consumption in a Southern African country, high-school graduates from the capital city were selected to carry out the survey because they had the necessary skills, and were available for hire. Both men and women were included. The study required several weeks of observation and data recording in a series of villages. The villagers were not willing to cook for the researchers, so the research coordinator provided the research teams with wood for cooking, utensils, and basic foods. In the event, the young men proved unwilling and unable to cook for themselves, having never done it before, and tended to drink beer and smoke instead. In order to ensure the survey, which had a tight deadline, was completed, the research coordinator was reduced to cooking food and transporting it to the men. The women researchers proved willing and able to cook for themselves, and also proved much more conscientious as field researchers. They seemed to have a greater stake in showing how well they could do the work. The research coordinator, a European woman, resolved that in future projects of a similar nature she would hire women in preference to men, because of their greater independence and reliability.

Styles of research

'Styles' is not quite the right word, but it is difficult to find a better one. Briefly, there are two sets of contrasts in the ways people organise research: the quantitative/qualitative split; and the formal/informal split. Instead of trying to be exhaustively systematic in discussing these, we shall simply suggest how the issues are related by looking at a single example.

Policy makers who must commit large sums of public money to social policy issues are aware that mistakes may mean both wasted money and social disruption or blighted lives. Consider the problem of working out accurately how many primary-school teachers will be needed for a particular region in ten years' time. Since family sizes are liable to change, a serious over-estimate would mean that teachers are trained and schools are built but with no children to occupy the places or the teachers. Result: wasted money, and frustrated, unemployed teachers. But a serious underestimate would mean shortages of school places, and of qualified teachers, with bad effects on the quality of primary-school education for the unlucky children. Therefore, precise predictive, quantitative research is needed to get the calculations right. This must also be research employing formal research methods — particularly the sample survey as a data-gathering device, and statistical analysis via computer software programmes.

But in the earlier, exploratory phase of this research, it will be necessary to ask married couples some searching questions about how many children they plan to have. This is a notoriously difficult area to research, but it is safe to say that, in order to get some understanding of the factors which make people decide such personal matters, some lengthy, relaxed, open-ended conversations between sensitive researchers of the same gender as the respondents will be required. This means informal, qualitative research. Only when issues have been explored at leisure, in depth, and in an informal, conversational setting, will the researchers be able to formulate precise questions for the essential quantitative phase of the work.

Note that in this case, informal and qualitative work is the essential pre-cursor for the formal, quantified phase. Each depends upon the other for over-all predictive accuracy. The methods are not in competition — they are appropriate for different phases of the total research exercise. How does this relate to development project research? Scaling down from country to province or district, the satisfactory expenditure of development funds (even more scarce than tax revenue because raised by voluntary contributions from people who have already paid taxes), requires equal sensitivity and rigour. Development programmes are guided by the notion of equity, or fairness. Programmes are aimed at the most vulnerable and needy social groups, and can only reach those targets if such groups are correctly identified. Development funds which miss the poorest and help make the rich richer are seriously wasted. They are not only failing to do what they were meant to do, but they may also be strengthening local power structures. Therefore, the accuracy of targeting — involving the correct identification of the categories of people in need — is of essential importance.

As in the previous example, research on development issues has both quantitative and qualitative aspects. The same problems face NGOs as face national planners, but on a small canvas, and with the difference that NGO development researchers, who give priority to close consultation with and participation of local people, stand a better chance of designing projects which will work well and lead to local empowerment.

Development agencies, and large projects supported by these agencies, are increasingly employing programme staff from the countries in which they are operating. Involving these staff in research has two useful spin-offs. First, the local staff become better informed about the great variations in social and economic conditions, and the survival strategies of the poor, in their own countries. Secondly, the research experience gives them specific roles in contributing to the setting of objectives for the agency's annual workplan. Because they obtain direct experience of collecting and analysing the data and feeding research into the plan, they develop enhanced commitment to the achievement of programme objectives.

3 THE RANGE OF RESEARCH METHODS

Making the most of existing resources

Far too often people carry out new research without first checking what information already exists. There are many different sources of useful information, though the reliability and availability of particular sources will vary from country to country. More information is usually available than people initially believe. A degree of imagination is sometimes necessary in order to identify who or which office might possess useful information, and some lateral thinking can often pay enormous dividends when an invaluable source of information is uncovered. The most important point about checking out already existing information sources is that they are often either free or nearly free, and thus may save considerable sums from your 'new research' budget. Existing sources of information, sometimes called 'secondary sources', should always be checked before a commitment is made to new research and the collection of 'primary research data'.

Government statistics: National and local government departments often possess enormous piles of 'raw data' in the form of statistics which have often not been processed. These may have been collected for a multitude of reasons, but never published and sometimes not even analysed. For example, in a rural district of Peru information on trade in the district was obtained from a local police post which registered all trucks, and what they were carrying, which passed through a road block. A Ministry of Industry will often have data on all firms over a certain size; labour departments will register employers. It is surprising how often access can be obtained to such information by researchers; officials are often only too pleased that someone is finally using the information they laboriously collected! Many countries make statistical information available through a government publications office.

Census data form a particularly useful official source. Most (but not all) countries carry out national censuses at regular intervals, usually every tenth year in the series, 1951, 1961... Usually a Demographic Report is published summarising the data, or even providing access to all the raw materials collected in the census. A national statistical office will hold this material and be willing to make it available. It is worth investigating the form in which this material is held; some countries such as India publish several volumes of data on each census.

The questions asked in a census will vary considerably from country to country, from basic demographic enquiries to more sophisticated investigations of housing and employment. Whereas some questions are asked of everyone, other questions may be asked only from a sample of the population. It is important to know this and also to check the way the census was compiled: was it a full census of everyone in the country, or just an interim sample to update an earlier census? How well defined are the categories used in the sample? Are they overlapping? In Peruvian census data, for example, a child is classified as either *working* or *at school*. Although in reality a large number of children both work and go to school, this important fact is not shown in the census and indeed is actually obscured by its definitional categories. (This is a clear example of the census researchers having written one of their unresearched assumptions into the data collection and analysis!) So, census categories cannot be taken uncritically.

Census data can act as a useful cross-check. If you have made a survey of a district, you may be able to see if your results generally match those in the official census. A discrepancy may be informative. Perhaps it is explained by the two enquiries having been conducted at different times of the year, and the absence of young men in the national census may have been the result of short-term migration. If you find minor discrepancies but overall agreement about basics, you can be reassured that your own research has not missed something major.

Unpublished university manuscripts: Countless students throughout the world are obliged to write dissertations as part of their university course. Third World students will often write short studies of their own communities, or of another in which they have some contact through family or other connections. These can provide good sources of information on otherwise poorly-documented districts or communities, and may provide real insider knowledge, from the writer's commitment, and long familiarity with local people. An agency may contribute in small ways to the preparation of such research (use of photocopying equipment; access to agency library; financial contribution to research expenses) and in return get access to what may be a very helpful and insightful research document, and sometimes this can be much better value-for-money than buying a few days' work from an expatriate researcher. Some university libraries will keep these dissertations and index them, and can assist a search through them using a key word. Academics themselves will often be able to recommend particularly relevant pieces of work by their research students.

Other development agencies: Never assume that you are the first agency to have been concerned with the particular research problem — often other agencies will already possess studies, surveys, and reports on the same topic. Oxfam recently needed to review its programme in Yemen and obtained existing reviews of health and other problems in the country from two other international agencies.

Historical and anthropological research: Too many development agencies have a very short-term perspective about the people they are working with. Historical, ethnographic, and other related studies may provide a valuable insight into the development of a community and many clues to the characteristics and problems of a group. This material may sometimes enable you to challenge certain assumptions. For example, by comparing contemporary figures for population and agricultural production against information from the past, surprising insights may emerge: they may show whether a current crisis is indeed something contemporary or of a longer-term nature. You can also check whether people's cultural memories are accurate or not. In a particular area of Peru, peasants used to claim that they had possessed land since time immemorial but a check on historical records showed that they were descendants of immigrants brought to the area less than a hundred years ago. Similarly, an Amazonian tribal group in Ecuador turned out to be descendants of people brought from the highlands to work in the rubber plantations at the turn of the century; thus they were neither from the Amazon, tribal nor indigenous to the area!

Archives: Many societies possess local archives. In South America many important documents are held in privately-owned notary archives. In a rural area it is possible to piece together land records and other data from these archives. Ex-colonial countries may still have the colonial records, kept either in the independent state or by the former colonial power: an Eritrean researcher, for example, was able to use material held in Oxford at Rhodes House to study his country's agriculture. The quality, form, and organisation of archives will vary enormously. They may be almost forgotten and require some detective work to locate, or they may be organised so as to be highly accessible, but either way they are worth serious attention and can often prove a crucial source of invaluable information.

Published literature: It may seem obvious that you should check what has already been published on the area to be studied, but often the shelf-life of specialised publications may be very short and the print run very small. It is not always easy to locate books even a few years after they have been published. Where public libraries are not well developed, it may be necessary to find individuals with private libraries. And it is unfortunately true that it is often necessary to go outside a country in order to get information on that country. The large university libraries of Europe and the US may be far better stocked than those of the country about which the books are written. It is often worth carrying out a library search in such libraries as they will probably have materials not available locally and their holdings may go back further in time, so obscure and early studies are more likely to be discovered this way. The Royal Anthropological Institute Library and some other specialised libraries now have computerised indexes which can be readily accessed through information networks.

Local records and land registries: There are all kinds of local offices which may hold registries of land titles; register births, deaths, marriages; register local firms, vehicles, animals, licences to trade, court cases, inheritances, etc. The accuracy of such registries will vary enormously, but they often provide a surprising amount of basic information which may be of use in your research. For example, in areas which have recently been opened up by a new road it may be possible to measure the impact of the road by reviewing the number of people registering land in the path of the road, or alternatively disputing existing ownership of land because of its increased value due to the road.

Maps and cartographic services: (See also Geographic Information Systems, in Appendix 3.) It is not uncommon to believe that an area is unmapped only to discover that detailed maps and aerial photos are indeed available but not widely so. In some countries, maps and aerial photos may be held by the military authorities and special permission may be required to get access to them, but this could be well worth the effort as it is beyond the capacity of most groups to attempt their own mapping on anything but a very crude basis. Other bodies such as oil companies may also have invested in detailed maps so it is worth checking before you assume that maps are not available. Satellite photography has ensured that for most parts of the world some form of map or aerial picture exists.

Newspapers: Some newspapers may still have their own private press archives, or occasionally a national library may have one; these can supply historical, political, business and other data.

People: It is worth looking for people who may be able to act as information sources. For example, ex-colonial administrators may have their own archives, diaries, or libraries; librarians may know where materials are held; ex-government officials, retired politicians, retired judges, ex-landlords may all have private materials which could be useful to you. Of particular value will be academics in the national universities familiar with your research region and/or your research problem. They are likely to be supervising postgraduate research students, and some of these may be willing and able to assist on your research project, both for the research experience they will acquire, and for the payments they should receive.

It is unlikely that any single one of these sources will provide all the information you need, but experience shows that they may well provide a great deal of material and save you the time of trying to collect it yourself. This secondary material can also be useful for cross-checking your own information and validating it (see later discussion of validation). By bringing together information from different sources you can begin to build up a data bank yourself, which you can index. The introduction of micro-computers with relatively cheap software makes this far easier than it used to be. Sometimes it can be worth publishing a guide to the materials you have located to make these source of information more accessible to other people and save them having to repeat all your own detective work. For example, some years ago researchers discovered the long-lost land titles of a peasant community in the highlands of Peru, which were essential if the community were to defend their land rights against competing claims. Materials you have identified should be left with local institutions to build up future research capacity. A recent Oxfam researcher in Lima produced an annotated bibliography for groups there, which was made available when she left on completion of her project.

The time spent on collecting secondary material is rarely wasted. It may actually save time by making primary research unnecessary, or enabling you to avoid mistakes later. One word of warning, however: research can become a fetish for some people; they restrict access to their ever-increasing store, without realising that information is only worth something if it is being used.

Asking questions and interviewing

Let us start by considering cultural differences. In certain places any question from a stranger can carry an aggressive or intrusive message, because it involves A requiring action from B. Some people do not mind this — in rural Greece and Cyprus, it is part of an enjoyable cultural 'game' for one villager to ask another questions, and the other to 'resist' giving specific answers:

> 'Where are you going?'
> 'Over there.'
> 'Where have you come from?'
> 'Back there...'

But both parties understand the game, and in a more sensitive context, if A asks B an intrusive question and B chooses not to answer, this is signalled by saying nothing, smiling, and waiting. No offence is taken, because to be silent is to resist, and to resist is to win the exchange. And that is just one constraint for verbal questions.

If a person goes around a village in a certain region with a clip-board, seeking written replies to a list of questions, many people will insist that they are 'too busy' to answer (even though they may spend much of the day playing cards, if it is a slack time of year), and describe the researcher as someone 'taking statements', the term used for a policeman seeking evidence about a crime. The whole question of writing things down may be very sensitive in a society where people are fearful of the authorities, or political militants; so the pressure against writing things down may lead you to select informal methods of inquiry — the casual conversation rather than the questionnaire, or the reassuringly anonymous group discussion, rather than working with anxious, insecure individuals one at a time.

There are some cultures in which people tend to avoid direct encounter and direct questions. In many parts of Asia it is considered very rude for a junior person to answer an inquiry from a senior person negatively, so the naive researcher is likely to collect a lot of highly misleading 'false positives'. A relatively isolated group in the Philippines (the Buid) are shifting cultivators living in forested hills. By European standards they would be thought shy in various ways. When two Buid are having a conversation, they typically do not sit face-to-face, but at an angle of 45 degrees to each other, each facing outwards and away from the other. The buttonholing interview methods of Europe, in which a stranger A asks B to answer questions for half an hour would do nothing but frighten the Buid away; and there are

53

many similar groups of quiet, peaceful peoples, who have adapted to external pressures by keeping to themselves, who have a similarly non-confrontational style of dealing with other people.

The implications of the Buid culture and conversational style for any kind of research which involves asking questions are serious. You could not expect to learn much about how the Buid think and feel without a proper introduction to them, through someone they knew and trusted, and without also spending many hours in their company. You would have to become a person whom they could perceive to be fully human, by their criteria. This might involve your being ready to eat the same food as they do, and also being prepared to give and receive gifts.

So, any form of asking questions needs to be tailored to the cultural perceptions of the group in question, and this applies to the slightly more formal method of asking questions we call 'interviewing'. Clearly, the interview overlaps in certain respects with the questionnaire or survey, which will be considered in a later section, and it is less a distinctive method than a technique which can be used within several methods. At one end of a spectrum of person-to-person enquiries, with a person who initiates the questioning and a respondent, we can find formal, explicit, overt, and systematic methods, where written answers to specific questions are obtained (the standard survey); and at the other end from this, the most informal, conversational and open-ended methods of inquiry, with nothing being written down; with all kinds of mixes in between. All these procedures are commonly and loosely called 'interviews'.

At the most informal and unstructured end of the spectrum, A is conversing with B and allowing the material sought to 'emerge' from the conversation as and when B touches upon the issues A is interested in. This takes time, and patience, and B may never touch on what A wants to know.

A might change gear, and go for more directed questioning, although still in an informal style, with no note-taking and relying upon memory to capture B's answers. One further step in formalisation and comparability is reached if A has a small list of questions, jotted down on a half sheet of paper, and raises these from time to time with B, and later on with C, D, E, etc. The answers, too, may be roughly noted, without the whole process assuming burdensome or threatening proportions. These methods might be most appropriate for sensitive material, or hesitant informants.

As the methods get closer to the formal questionnaire, the questions become more specific, and systematic, and without any conversational intervals. The questions may also involve prompting the respondent into specific types of answers, as when the questioner says: *'Which of these statements best describes your own situation?':*

1. *I am never ill.*

2. *I am rarely ill.*

3. *I am often ill.*

4. *I am constantly ill.*

And the more precisely the responses are written down in full, and codified, the more streamlined and 'comparable' the answers become, and the more amenable to computer analysis, if that is desired.

Group interviews
It will be almost impossible to hold a group interview using closed questions. The aim of group interviews in part will be to encourage a collective response and to identify differences of opinion as well as areas of consensus within the group. A group interview is less likely to be successful where the members of the group are not reasonably homogeneous, as they will be inhibited and feel uncomfortable with each other if they are aware of major differences of status, class, or gender perspectives amongst them. The group interview can be a valuable way of quickly establishing some basic common ground, information and questions for future investigation.

Oral testimony, oral histories and life-histories
Most human societies have got along without literacy until recently, and illiterate people make better use of memory than do people who have come to rely on writing as a technique for storing information. Even in highly literate societies there is much important information which is not committed to paper,

and in recent years in Europe there have been a range of community-based movements to record the memories of ordinary people about the world they have grown up in, which has borne fruit in the writing of many local histories which are also vivid personal testimonies.

There is every reason to use local memories as research data. Sahelian pastoralists, for example, are very clear about long-term patterns of relatively good rainfall, and its alternation with dryer periods. They also remember the major famines in their own lifetimes and those they have heard about from older people. They are in a position to tell researchers about regeneration of vegetation, in areas where to the uninformed eye 'environmental degradation' has been 'irreversible'; and had aid agencies known how to listen to these oral testimonies they might have avoided some costly mistakes in recent interventions.

Another example of the value of non-written sources is land ownership, which is often not a matter of registered titles and fences, but of the memory of local elders, and the identification of particular trees, rocks, river-beds and other features of the terrain as boundary markers. The Giriama people on the Kenya coast have well-established methods for adjudicating between conflicting land claims, by calling on the oral testimony of disinterested elders. This sort of information can obviously be useful to development researchers, and it complements the emerging picture of non-literate people possessing elaborate collections of plant, animal, crop, land-use, and medicinal knowledge, much of which is of great practical value and is highly accurate and perceptive when considered as part of local adaptations to the particular climate, and environment. People from industrial societies, having had their attention caught by some traditional beliefs and practices which are either wrong, or even harmful by the standards of international scientific thought, are only now learning to pay proper attention to the much larger stores of local knowledge which are accurate and effective by those same international scientific standards.

There are two different 'pure' types of life-history. In the researcher-led type, there may be a list of 'prompting' questions, which elicit from the subject the sorts of issues which the investigator thinks are of importance for the research. For example, in researching about child-labour, an investigator might ask a person how old they were when they first started work, and to list the kinds of work they did, and the rewards if any, and to get through this work-history in as much detail as possible. The resulting narrative will appear to be 'all about work', but this will in one sense, be the outcome of the research method. The informant, without such directed prompting, would probably give a very different view of her life, emphasising caring for parents and children as the main 'theme'.

By contrast, in an informant-led life-history, the researcher might simply ask informants to give an outline of their lives in an undirected, open-ended way, thus allowing them to put the emphases on the things they themselves regarded as most significant. Such an approach can be very time-consuming, with a confident, articulate informant who has a lot to say, but with a shy informant, it may result in a very brief set of remarks which lack detail or highlights.

In practice, much life-history research is a mixture of the two, but it is methodologically sensible to be aware that you may get a rather different view of a sensitive issue if you prompt than if you do not.

In a recent study the development agency SOS Sahel interviewed 500 Sahelians, men and women, in eight different countries. Pastoralists and farmers were interviewed, as were fishermen. Refugees, both political and economic were also included in the study. The intention of the research was to discover the perceptions of the Sahelians themselves of the vital issues concerning the way their livelihood and environment had changed during their own lifetimes.

> Farmers talked about tried and tested methods of soil fertility, pastoralists explained how they control animal reproduction, the pastures preferred by each of their animals and the ideal ratio of males to females. Healing methods and herbal remedies are mentioned in varying degrees of detail.

Cross, N. and Barker, R. *At the Desert's Edge* Panos Institute/SOS Sahel 1991

The character of the recent changes is discussed and elaborated. After reading the book, no visiting specialist from outside the Sahel could be naive about the perceptiveness and resilience of the Sahelians, and their eloquent testimonies will do much to make the nature of their problems immediately clear to people from very different backgrounds.

Some tribal groups have faithfully recorded not only the legends of their societies but also such things as hunting techniques as a cultural record which they feel helps them maintain a pride in their culture and avoids it being lost as a consequence of external pressures. The Shuar Federation of Ecuador has an impressive library of booklets based on transcribing oral memories and knowledge to paper. The sources of oral material will be varied but may include songs, drama, stories, nursery rhymes, or rituals. It is often possible to interview old people, or local religious specialists, who may act as repositories of the community's oral history and memory. Local people will be able to say who is particularly knowledgeable and reliable.

This short discussion on oral traditions should remind you that you should always be on the look out for unexpected sources of information — never assume that there is none to be had. Always treat with some scepticism those who claim that information does not exist about a certain community.

One final point, which applies to all the research methods discussed in this book: all information is partial, with particular emphases, and omissions. And all memories contain local cultural assumptions, rather than being simply factual. No-one is ever wholly truthful, in the sense of remembering everything accurately. To take an example close to home: any ordinary telephone user, asked to list all the phone calls s/he have made or received over the last 48 hours, will typically only recall about 50 per cent of the total — the ones they regarded as particularly important. Oral testimonies tend to be 'edited highlights' of a person's experience, and should be given no greater (but no lesser) credence than any other kind of information produced by people, and extracted by researchers.

Surveys

The survey (also known as the sample survey employing a questionnaire) is the best method for certain specific tasks, but not for others. In essence, a survey involves asking a series of formal questions of selected people, writing down their responses, and subsequently analysing them. A survey aims to give systematic, representative and reliable information about a particular set of people, the research population. If a Ministry of Agriculture needs to know what fruit trees farming men and women would wish to plant around their dwellings, or a health department needs to find out what are the most prevalent life-threatening diseases in a particular district, then some form of survey will be the preferred method of getting the most reliable answers.

A survey can yield reliable results when it asks people about matters they do not find too private or threatening, and to which they can give fairly definite answers. It is not the best method for gathering information about private or otherwise sensitive matters because interviewers employed to conduct surveys might not be trusted with sensitive information, either because they are strangers to the respondents or because they are members of the same community, and might be thought tempted to gossip, or use the information for personal advantage. Among the topics which are likely to be too sensitive for survey work would be political loyalties, debts, and sexual practices (particularly if they go against the moral or religious norms of the community). Such matters require more informal research methods, where the researcher has over time built up a relationship of trust with the respondent. (See the section on Participant Observation p. 63.)

The first phase of survey research is normally qualitative interviewing, where one of the team asks a small number of informants to talk at length about the issues the survey will be concerned with. This enables the researchers to understand the issues in the terms in which they are familiar to the informants. Researchers may need to elicit the information by non-directive 'probe' questions, such as 'Tell me all the problems you face about water in this community...' or 'What are the matters which most concern you about your childrens' health?' These interviews may be allowed to run for an hour or more with each informant, and might be tape-recorded for ease of reference. If during this phase the same issues are raised with each informant, some preliminary regularities in response may emerge.

After these qualitative or 'in depth' interviews have been discussed among the team of researchers, it should be possible to produce a first attempt at a questionnaire, to be 'piloted' — that is, field-tested to remove all sources of weakness and error. The precise wording of the questions and the order in which they are asked require attention, because it is all too easy to ask questions which are either ambiguous and will be misunderstood by some respondents or which lead to unhelpful answers. Particular care should be taken to use words, idioms, and grammar which will be readily understood by local people. These details are best worked out in the pilot phase, because otherwise time and resources will be wasted. (Appendix 2 gives two versions of a short questionnaire, with forms of the questions compared, and an explanation in each case for why one form is to be preferred to the other.)

Sampling

A survey may be complete, covering the whole target population, or incomplete, when the population is large and it would cost too much time, money and effort to question everyone. If incomplete, then some form of sample will need to be made. There are many kinds of sampling methods and a good deal of information is necessary before deciding on which method to use. Here, we do no more than point to a few frequently-used methods.

Deciding on the size of sample you need requires some expert guidance — there is no simple rule of thumb, because the sample size is related to how accurate you need to be, the character of the population and what you already know about it, and how much time, money, and energy you can spend. *Social Survey Methods, Development Guidelines 6*, by Paul Nichols, published by Oxfam in 1991, has been specially written to help with the practical problems development workers face in carrying out surveys.

One kind of sample is the simple random sample. Suppose you have 350 people and you decide to interview 20 per cent of them. If you have an accurate, up-to-date list of their names, you can give each name a number. Take a roll of tickets numbered 1 to 350, and put them into a box, and after shaking them about, draw 70 tickets, and interview the persons identified by these numbers.

Alternatively, you could decide to use a systematic sample, and interview every fifth person on the list, providing there was no reason to suppose that some systematic distortion might creep in. How could this happen? It is unlikely, but possible: suppose you were working your way through a large planned settlement, or a block of flats. It might be that units were built in two sizes, small and large, and that they were grouped in sets of four small, then one large. If you chose every fifth house, you might unintentionally 'hit' all the big houses!

A stratified random sample is used when you know in advance that the population in question contains a number of non-overlapping sub-groups (the 'strata' of the method's name). For example, suppose you were interested in farmers' outputs, and farmers grew the same crop in three different ecological zones. Then you might decide to take a random sample of farmers within each of the three zones, keeping the sample proportionate in size: if there were 220 farmers in one zone (stratum), and you were doing a 5 per cent sample, you would calculate 5 per cent of 220, which is 11. You would then use a random method (numbered tickets) to select 11 farmers to interview from the 220; then repeat the exercise for farmers from the other two zones.

The methods just mentioned are all examples of random sampling, which can be used when for one reason or another you possess, or can produce, an entire listing of the population to be studied. But if this is unavailable and impractical you will need to use a non-random sampling method, and one of the most commonly used methods is called 'quota sampling'. This requires that you understand some of the important distinctions within your research population, even though you do not have a complete listing of the individuals. The interviewers are each given a 'quota' of different types of people to interview, representative of the population as a whole, and use their own judgement in selecting people to make up their quota.

If you do not have a full listing of the research population, and you have no independent description of them, such as a census, to allow you to know how to stratify a sample, or how to select quotas, then you are 'stuck'. One way forward would be to do a systematic sample of, say, every 20th household, and derive a baseline description from this survey, and use it for any further refinements needed.

The pros and cons of a survey

Surveys are useful for obtaining factual or attitudinal information about large populations, especially in the absence of alternative information, where are there many unanswered 'how many ' type of questions. Unfortunately, many researchers feel surveys are the only way of producing useful and scientifically acceptable information. In fact they can be a slow and clumsy way of obtaining information which could be obtained more easily and more cheaply. So, before mounting a survey, think about alternative methods of obtaining the information you need.

In certain cases, for example where questions of health are concerned, a survey may be the only way of establishing a baseline of health data for an area, and can also provide an important way in which local people can work out their health priorities and affordable solutions in the absence of an existing health service. But the survey will only be one element of the research exercise, and the community-wide discussion of its findings will be the most significant phase. Similarly, a plan to provide a service such as water may require an accurate estimate of the number of potential users. However, many surveys collect far too much information because there is a tendency to add extra questions to the survey document, leading to long unwieldy questionnaires, which then merely create problems when it comes to analysing the data. If a survey is too long, informants get bored and irritated while it is being carried out, and the word will get around the community, producing higher rates of non-response.

Rather than trying to tie all information collection into one grand survey, it will often be more useful to carry out a range of mini-surveys to cover specific areas of concern. This will have the advantage that each issue will be more manageable, and that as one mini-survey is analysed it may give a lead to the next set of information needs, thus retaining more flexibility than an exercise which requires all questions and alternatives to be foreseen at the time of designing the questionnaire.

Finally, here are some questions to ask yourself before deciding to carry out a survey:

Have the beneficiaries been properly consulted, and has the nature and purpose of the survey been fully explained to them?

Can the project really afford the time and energy?
Will the survey provide accurate and comprehensive answers to the important research and policy questions?
Can the beneficiaries themselves analyse the data? If they cannot, can you? Or can you find someone who can?
When and how will the pilot be done? And how will the results of the survey be communicated to the beneficiaries?

Participant observation

Participant observation is a method widely used by anthropologists, rural sociologists, and human geographers. It entails the researcher becoming resident in a community for a period of many months and observing the normal daily lives of its members. Where possible, researchers try to live within a local household and participate in routine production activities. The extent to which an outsider can be fully accepted into a community is the subject of lively debate. Some researchers seek to conform closely to local customs and, although they are rarely prepared to undergo painful initiation ceremonies, they will attend weddings and funerals, make appropriate gifts, and become increasingly accepted by their closest informants whom they end up regarding as friends. Other researchers prefer to retain greater personal autonomy and, while residing in a community, live by themselves and conform far less to local mores.

By residing in the community, it becomes possible to collect information more slowly and informally, through observation rather than through formal surveys, indirect questions rather than questionnaires. The researcher will normally record information in notebooks, on a day-to-day, topic-by-topic basis, but making concentrated studies of particular phases of crop production, religious ritual or political debate as they occur.

The earlier anthropologists used to study everything which happened, by a kind of vacuum-cleaner technique. Modern anthropology has become increasingly specialised, and fieldworkers start their research with detailed lists of factual and theoretical questions they wish to answer over the course of a year or more. They have coherent long-term research plans, even though on an hour-to-hour or day-to-day basis they are prepared to operate informally, flexibly and opportunistically.

The disadvantages of participant observation are that it is slow and intensive. First, there is research training and language acquisition; then there is sustained fieldwork; lastly there is the analysis of the copious material collected. A novice may need several years before being ready to make an in-depth report. Participant observation is only as good as the observer: the findings may reflect the researcher's social context and research pre-occupations in such a way that the material is not helpful or accessible to people outside the scholarly field.

It can be very difficult to cross-check the participant observer's findings because the specific time of the field research, the network of personal contacts, and the research framework employed may together mean that another researcher could not in any simple sense 'reproduce' the first study. Social life cannot be 'repeated' in the way a laboratory experiment with controlled variables can be repeated. Some observers become so involved in the culture they have been observing, and absorbed by the minute details of the community and its inner life, that they have little interest in more general questions.

The advantages of participant observation are that it can provide a well-rounded and well-founded picture of the community. Someone resident in the community can observe aspects of the lives of households and individuals throughout the week, month, and year. This avoids the seasonal biases of so many research methods, as well as the fragmentary insights produced by short visits when visitors may be given special treatment. It is one of the best ways of understanding the dynamics of power relationships, particularly as between women and men, within households and other groups. Political and economic leverage are often only visible when the slower processes of social life can be followed through, in fine detail.

Participant observation is particularly useful in collecting information on groups with whom contact is difficult to achieve during a short or formal visit, particularly low-status groups, or those with a defensive outlook. The method can encourage trust to develop between the researcher and a community to such an extent that the researcher can move through the community and talk to members far more freely than would otherwise be possible. By being in the community all the time the researcher becomes a part of the scenery and no longer a threat or a novelty. This advantage allows far better contact with women, for example, or minorities within the community. It allows the researcher to get past the self-appointed community 'spokesmen' (frequently men), and come to know a much wider spectrum of people, young and old, female and male, influential and disregarded.

Participant observation is not going to be very useful where answers to certain basic questions are required quickly for the purposes of programme interventions. But it is possible to adapt the techniques of participant observation within a wider research programme in order to validate ideas and findings from other methodologies. You can ask a sympathetic social researcher, who is about to do field work in pursuit of their own research concerns, to look out for certain relationships (share-cropping, debt-bondage), keep diaries, report on local issues, and so forth; but this should not involve asking someone to step outside their normal role, or confuse it. A community could distrust an extension worker who started asking questions about matters outside the agricultural sphere; and an anthropologist may wish to preserve his or her independence while in the field, and be unwilling to take on additional questions.

We said that an apprentice anthropologist may need several years from start of training to readiness to present an analysis of field data. But once anthropologists have completed their first major fieldwork, and written it up, they become much more confident, and efficient. With a good knowledge of the language and a network of close contacts, an anthropologist on a follow-up visit to a community may be able to produce high-quality insights into specific questions very quickly, and with much greater reliability than most outsiders. You might save yourself a lot of research time if you can identify an experienced anthropologist who has worked in the project area, whom you can then commission to undertake a short-term purposive study to meet your needs.

Appendix 6 gives a description of modified participant-observation, an 'Action Research Programme', carried out by local researchers for a relatively short period of time. As they were mostly locals, they had the advantage of local language proficiency and could therefore get useful results quickly.

Rapid Rural Appraisal

Rapid Rural Appraisal or Assessment (RRA) is a method of grass-roots research used to identify the problems, goals and strategies of households, groups and communities. It is a fairly new arrival on the research scene, devised to meet the special needs of development-oriented research when decisions have to be made in a time-frame of months rather than years. It is a relatively low-cost approach to collecting information quickly, which came into existence precisely because the slower time-frame of apprentice anthropologists, and their reluctance to give priority to 'applied' questions at the expense of their own interests, meant there was an information-gap in development project research. When development workers tried to remedy this themselves, they often fell into a series of bias-traps:

Tarmac-bias: they visited communities which were too near to a good road to be typical.

Dry-season bias: they travelled in the dry season, when movement is easy.

Elite-bias: they were often guided by staff who were members of or related to the national elite, who would tend to show them things which reflected well on the national government.

Male-bias: they tended to be guided by a man, and introduced to senior male community leaders, who told them what they thought the women thought.

Site-bias: too often, what these 'development tourists' saw were things that project staff chose for them; they did not make their own site decisions.

Rapid Rural Appraisal was developed to prevent these biases distorting applied research, but to do so without the necessity for the year-long immersions of the field anthropologists. The RRA approach uses existing knowledge and experience to address issues directly, and is employed by inter-disciplinary teams working with project staff and in regular contact with the local population. There is normally a problem-focus on practical and policy-oriented questions which need answering. The objective is not 'understanding for its own sake' but the pursuit of understanding which will lead to action.

RRA favours team-work over the 'lone ranger' approach. Five heads are better than one because they can marshall more insights, check each other's biases, generate imaginative ideas for furthering the task in hand, and give moral support during periods of intensive and demanding research.

RRA is flexible: it allows for constant feedback to the original research questions, and changes to the research agenda, as needed. It should prevent researchers getting locked into the wrong questions and thus wasting time and money. RRA prefers the concrete and the actual over the abstract and hypothetical. It sets great store by the respondents' perceptions, and deals with specifics rather than generalities. It favours visual aids to elicit information, and guide groups through process-questions.

Having said all this, we are not in a position to present a recipe for how to carry out a RRA: there is no magic method, in powder form, to which you can add water, and stir! It is not so much a method or methods, more an outlook, and a requirement to produce useful results to a deadline which is weeks or months away. The RRA approach was devised in particular to help rapid assessment of projects covering a number of different activities over large areas in a limited time span. It relies heavily upon the use of interviews and observation by a combination of project staff and professionals. The professionals should be conversant with the type of work being reviewed, but there is no particular discipline which defines the core method, and anyone can make a valid contribution. In one sense, RRA is like good investigative journalism and involves an imaginative and intelligent use of common sense, put to specified goals. It may be necessary to complement the data collected through RRA with other information from surveys, and existing materials.

The emphasis on RRA's being a team activity is a control against personal biases. If a group of five women and men go out each day, all looking at the same set of issues, and comparing notes each evening, the chances of unconscious personal biases resulting in distorted selective perceptions are reduced, though never entirely eliminated.

One common RRA approach is the compilation of check lists. On one side will be listed the objectives of the project in the case of an appraisal or evaluation, on the other side comments and observations will be added as a result of the informal interviews or observations. The two sides of the page or sheets are then compared to see whether there is a match or not. For example one objective of a project might include provision of more accessible clean water, and solid waste disposal. If observations made while walking through the area show large numbers of women still carrying water pots on their heads, and piles of rubbish rotting on street corners, then it becomes sensible to question how successful the project has been in meeting its objectives. Follow-up could be direct questions to women about water access and a closer look at the activities of community-paid garbage collectors.

Such a direct approach only works if there is something to compare the current results with. In our example, it is possible that however bad things are now, they were significantly worse before the project started. Even more women might have been carrying water, from longer distances, and the rubbish might have been piled even higher. But the local people themselves should be able to give a useful insight to such a straightforward issue, by including a question at the end of the list which focuses on change: 'In your view, is the situation with regard to water access the same as it was a year ago? Or better? Or worse? '

One of the commonest RRA procedures, borrowed from psychology, is ranking tasks. If the researcher is trying to find out which sorts of trees local farmers would prefer to have available from a government nursery, then the procedure will have two phases. First, farmers would be asked to list the trees they would like, and this could be done slowly and informally, with each tree type being noted in the order in which it is mentioned. But later, with either the same group or another group, the names of trees could be read out to the farmers in a list, and they could be asked to state which would be their 'favourite', their second, and their third preferred tree. In this way, both the total list of trees and the preference for particular trees would have come from the farmers themselves, and the two-phase procedure would help offset the sort of bias which arises from asking people to name their three favourite trees, in a way which seems to pressurise them to make quick and simple decisions.

In more complex programmes with varied and hard-to-measure objectives, such comparisons will be more difficult. If there are base-line indicators of poverty, child malnutrition, tenant-indebtedness, then some kind of 'before-and-after' comparison might be attempted. But without any base-line data there is a danger that the method is little more than the subjective perspective of the observer who uses an experienced eye to gauge or 'guesstimate' the direction of change — measuring wealth by the number of television aerials, or lack of them, the presence of articles such as bicycles and so forth, in a community.

In short, by carrying out RRA, you can avoid collecting too much data through more expensive means. Many costly surveys yield masses of data which remain effectively unanalysed, and so become an expensive 'white elephant'. RRA provides a framework which avoids the dangers of 'development tourism' — the collection of information on short-term visits, with an arbitrary selection of sites and persons encountered. It is a corrective to individual biases, and can be used to encourage the participation of local people in the research process.

The variety of RRA techniques

The combination of techniques used will depend upon the circumstances and staff/resource availability. These are some of the most common techniques:

Investigation of existing secondary material: This is fully described in the previous section (pp.47-52).

Direct field observations: These should prevent certain 'naive assumptions' from desk-bound theorists from becoming influential in project design. Testing out all practical proposals with local people will often uncover objections and bottlenecks which have never occurred to the planners.

Semi-structured interviews: These involve using a check list of questions and issues, rather than a questionnaire, and encouraging a mixture of people to respond. It is particularly important to get out of the village committee-room, or the community-leader's control, and meet people in the fields, at the well, in the cooking area or wherever else they spend their day.

Group interviews: Allowing people to respond informally in a group discussion. The groups should be fairly homogeneous, so that people feel comfortable and able to speak freely.

Informal workshops with local people: These can include 'brainstorming', discussions, and problem-solving exercises, and are ways of getting groups to identify issues, problems, successes and failures in a relatively quick and public way. If people argue with each other, the arguments will be informative, and by allowing people to 'have their say' may help everyone to see where future problems lie.

Ranking exercises: These involve asking people to place their own priorities in order of importance. An example would be when, having first elicited an open-ended list of village needs, people are shown the list and asked: 'What is the most important thing your village needs? The second most? The third most? The least?'

Role-playing exercises: These can allow people to articulate their feelings and problems in an unstructured way, and an RRA team can use this technique to elicit discussion and comments from respondents.

Sketch-maps, transects, diagrams, and other visual aids: These can all help to make contexts more concrete, highlight relations, and keep the salient features of a situation fresh and easy-to-remember.

There are other techniques which can be used, but all have in common the attempt to elicit information from local people, which is focused on their practical concerns, and which is in some sense objectified, so that it can be compared and assessed. The simple technique of asking informants to spell out what is good and what is bad about a new crop, a farming method, a health clinic, or a dam proposal can bring specific problems quickly into the open. The range of possible methods which can be employed by RRA groups is open-ended, and enthusiasts are suggesting new procedures all the time.

Collating and presenting RRA findings

One of the challenges to people using an RRA approach is how to collate the different findings, comments, observations and other materials. The advantage of having used different techniques is that it allows for cross-validation (some people call this 'triangulation'). This consists of cross-checking different opinions or observations and it allows incomplete pieces of information to be completed by 'intelligent guesswork'. For example, if a full survey of water use was carried out in one village, this can be extrapolated to the other five villages in the area, especially where local comments from these villages on water usage were compatible with the survey results by indicating similarities between them.

The initial findings from an RRA exercise should be shared with the local people in order to cross-check their accuracy and allow for amendments before any final report is written.

Limitations of RRA

The danger of RRA allowing individual bias a clear field is usually prevented by its normally being a team activity. The biggest questions arise where clear objectives or base-line data do not exist. RRA should be a technique which is complementary to other methods which have preceded it or which will follow on. It is least reliable when employed in isolation. In general, the bigger the possible expenditure, or the more vital the issue to local people, the less it is advisable to build a major policy on RRA alone. RRA cannot ever be as accurate as more thorough methods, so it produces at best an estimate rather than a fully-supportable conclusion or answer. In addition, because it is carried out as a one-off exercise, RRA usually produces a static view of the long and slow process of development, and can easily fall prey to seasonal and other biases.

Some of the RRA techniques available may not be appropriate in certain cultural and political environments. If local women are hesitant about talking to strange visiting men, a RRA team of four men and one woman is obviously going to be weak on cross-checking the woman researcher's observations.

An example of a RRA

In one well-documented example of a RRA, the problem chosen was to ascertain what determined fluctuations in yield of sugar cane farmed in Fiji. Yields in Fiji are typically lower than many other cane-producing regions, and an understanding of this could help local producers. The author identified four procedures for gathering and filtering information, and for focusing upon relevant factors:

Secondary data reviewing: consulting previous reports, research documents, photographs, maps, and anything else to form an overview, and identify gaps in information.

Semi-structured interviewing: informal discussions with local people with specialist knowledge, particularly farming households. Direct observation of conditions, procedures and equipment, to complement the interviews.

Workshops: bringing together everyone involved in the production process to discuss, analyse and develop the findings of the RRA team. During the secondary data review, a series of hypotheses were formed and grouped under several headings. These were:

Environmental conditions;
Farming practices;
Causes of poor farming practices;
Problems of the sugar cane industry.

To facilitate interviewing, cartoon-like drawings were produced which showed different stages of cane production, and these were used to assist interviewers in asking specific questions about the time of year and labour requirements for each stage. After rapport had been established, such devices were no longer so necessary, but they were useful 'ice-breakers'.

Diagrams were produced analysing the organisational relationships between the Fiji Sugar Corporation and the growers. Other diagrams related the seasons to climate and rainfall conditions, and the labour requirements of production. As the RRA proceeded, some of the most important human factors which determined relative yield per hectare began to emerge, and these included farm size (whether or not it was large enough to yield a satisfactory income); availability of off-farm income; the number of healthy adults per household; and reciprocal labour arrangements with friends or relatives.

Later in the RRA process, a series of 15 essays were produced on varied aspects of cane farming. These were grouped as follows:

A General analyses
  1 Cane Farming in Fiji.
  2 Patterns of farming in Lovu [the survey area].
  3 Differences between Lovu growers.
  4 Growers' perceptions.
  5 Field officers' perceptions.

B Key factors investigated
  6 Cyclones and droughts.
  7 Rainfall in 'normal' climatic years.
  8 Poor management.
  9 Poor soil and slope.

C Key causal factors of poor management
  10 Causes of low fertiliser usage.
  11 Fijian village life [Koro village].
  12 Financial problems common to all growers.
  13 Small farm size.
  14 Large farms.
  15 The 'ideal' situation.

By the end of the RRA, it was established that small farms under 4 hectares tended to devote less labour to cane production and more to non-cane income, and were lower-yielding. The largest farms experienced high costs in employing additional labour, and if they had locational problems, were unlikely to be high-yielding on cane. The best yields were on medium-sized farms, where there was a good supply of family labour on an all-round basis. Cyclones and droughts were shown to cause very reduced yields. A number of recommendations were produced, each aimed at a specific unit: the field, the farm, the community, and the corporation. Further questions were opened up by the RRA for more intensive, policy-focused research.

(Source: McCracken J.A.(1988), 'A working framework for Rapid Rural Appraisal: lessons from a Fiji experience', *Agricultural Administration and Extension*, 29 pp.163-184.)

Participatory Rural Appraisal

Participatory Rural Appraisal (PRA) has grown out of cross-fertilisation between the emphasis on participation, and RRA. It has been developed by Robert Chambers, the Aga Khan Foundation, Action Aid, Oxfam and other agencies. While some of PRA's principles and procedures have been in existence for a long time, as a named research package it is a fairly new arrival on the scene.

Where RRA assumes that a team of specialists are responding to a problem identified in a local community, in PRA the goal is to shift the leadership of the project, and as much of the research work as possible, from the non-local visiting experts to local people themselves. In this way, power, the power to initiate and to implement, should shift away from the development agency towards the local community. It is this desire to shift power, or at the least, to share it more fully, which distinguishes PRA from RRA. Furthermore, PRA puts no premium on the speed of the research — on the contrary, its promoters stress the need for unhurried appraisal.

One characteristic PRA procedure involves the initiators, on entering a community, to spend some time trying their hands at standard local production tasks, such as chopping wood, ploughing, weeding, or irrigating — anything needing know-how and manual dexterity. They invite the local people to comment critically on the way they perform the tasks, and since they normally perform them clumsily, there is plenty of scope for them to be corrected. This 'ice-breaker' serves several purposes. First, it allows the villagers to see the visitors less as powerful, high-status people and more as vulnerable and fallible, particularly in terms of the locality and the skills it needs. This does not reduce everyone to permanent equality, but it should allow status differences to be temporarily suspended, and to be shown to be relative to contexts, and not absolute. From the visitors' point of view, the lesson is a reminder that the villagers are skilled people, who have survived in their environment through the development of locally-appropriate knowledge. Thus, the equation educated expert: villager = knowledgeable person: ignorant person is erased, and in its place is the suggestion that all knowledge is limited and provisional, more relevant to some contexts than others, and subject to revision.

One thing which PRA seems to be particularly good at is communicating the development perceptions of agency staff to locals, and vice versa. Because the two groups perform a number of basic data-gathering and data-analysis tasks together, confidence in mutual open-mindedness and ability to listen is established. PRA initiators like to use locally-available devices to make visible the outcomes of the data-gathering tasks. So, in an investigation of crop cultivation as a proportion of village land, a map of the village land might be drawn in sand or dust (or sketched) with different crop items placed on the map to signify the different areas in which they are cultivated. This 'visualisation' of village productivity might help assure the locals that the visitors have got a good idea of the things which matter most to the villagers. Mistakes can be readily corrected, and no loss of face, or significant waste of resources is involved. Nor, in these simple procedures, is anyone bedazzled by high-tech equipment.

Many of the procedures and techniques already discussed in connection with RRA — wealth ranking tasks, sketch-mapping the local community and its resources, discussion groups to assess causes and solutions to local problems — are used in PRA under the non-directive guidance of trainers, or activators; but with the conscious goal of encouraging the local people to experiment, to analyse, to suggest solutions, and as far as possible to take the major initiatives for whatever they decide they need.

Perhaps one of the most valuable opportunities to use PRA is in a situation where a series of local communities are in conflict over resource management. In such a case, PRA may be adapted to produce mediation procedures. By mapping land-use areas, and the needs for different groups to have access to a variety of resources, previously hostile groups can come to see the pressures on those with whom they are in dispute. From there it may be possible for the groups concerned to propose and manage regulatory procedures which head-off future conflicts.

At present, PRA is still evolving, and even its most enthusiastic advocates are coming up with many questions about the method and its possible comparative advantages. The reader should refer back both to the RRA section, and to our earlier suggestion that perhaps the most important initial question to settle about participative methods is, do the community's most vulnerable people really wish to devote time and energy to the exercise? Can definite benefits to them be reliably predicted?

It seems likely that PRA as a method will be most effective where the training and funding agency is already well-known to the local group, and has gained trust through years of association and a proven track record of sensitive assistance. But where an agency, or its operating staff, is new to the community, it might be advisable to wait before introducing PRA methods until a relationship has been developed, and in the meantime, employ some of the better-tried research methods already discussed.

The PRA approach seems most likely to produce positive results, in terms of a successfully mobilised local community prepared to see a project through, if the project involves something which can be clearly seen to benefit the whole community, or at least a large majority of people, without harming anyone — for example, a project to improve the health of everyone in the local community, by means of a series of public-health measures supported by the training of local health workers. (If there were practising local healers who stood to lose by the new procedures, they would need to be integrated into the project and their livelihoods assured.) Provided no-one stands to lose by the project, or has an interest in blocking it, the desirability of the benefits may act to secure commitments of time and energy. Similarly, a project aimed at dealing with a local environmental or threatened resource problem, such as uplands soil erosion silting up a major irrigation tank, may command wide support.

However, it seems clear that PRA in and of itself cannot remove major conflicts of interest, or dissolve structural inequalities, and for this reason it remains one research method among many, or, in its other role as a means of community-activation, a procedure which will work well for some communities and tasks, but not for others.

4 GENERAL ISSUES AFFECTING MOST RESEARCH METHODS

The use of appropriate indicators

There are several different kinds of indicators which can be used for monitoring and evaluation, and provide a way of comparing and 'ranking' different groups. The most common form of indicator is economic. Most statistics on poverty are related to income in some way or another. At the macro level of national accounts we still compare countries by their 'Gross National Product'. At a micro level, different ways are used to calculate relative wealth and poverty. One apparently straightforward way is to calculate the income earned and capital owned by an individual or group. In reality it may be extremely difficult to get clear information on cash income, other entitlements (remittances, pensions, food directly consumed), or capital such as the amount of land or animals owned.

Wealth ranking is a way in which comparative poverty/wealth can be judged. It is done by getting people from a group under study to make their own list of their neighbours' relative wealth. The names of families (or individuals/heads of households) from the community are written on separate file cards, then people are asked to put the cards into order starting with the richest family and finishing with the poorest. The exercise is repeated with all the members of the group, or a sample. The individual results are then collated by the researcher, and the average score obtained by each family determines their respective place in the final wealth/poverty index.

In the 1960s one school of North American anthropology relied heavily upon the use of 'cultural indicators' to assess levels of 'development'. Such indicators included whether a village had a hairdresser, or other specialist shops, whether people gave streets names, whether they used indigenous forms of dress or 'western' clothes, and so on. This type of indicator is more indicative of the researchers' own biases than informative about the people being studied.

There are alternative ways of allowing a group to agree their own 'cultural' indicators of progress, which are useful as a means of judging their perceptions of whether they have experienced some progress or not, or some level of material improvement or the opposite. For example, in some nomadic groups who set great store by hospitality, poverty is often indicated by members of the community by referring to the lack of coffee to offer visitors, rather than increased malnutrition of the children or their own hunger. In another area in rural Ecuador a poor Indian group cited the building of a church in their community as a sign that they had overcome their previous dominance by the local 'mestizo' township.

In the evaluation of social development programmes one of the major difficulties encountered by evaluators is in the definition of indicators which can be used as means of measuring the progress, or lack of it, made by social development programmes. It is not always easy to choose indicators which can be used to judge the improved level of 'awareness' or 'self-confidence' of individuals and groups of people. One way of choosing such indicators is to allow a group to identify its own indicators. They may then refer to more obvious things like the number of times they feel able to stand up and speak openly in village meetings, or more subtle changes like the diminished use by local shop-keepers of the diminutive when referring to customers from a local indigenous group. (For more discussion of the use of indicators in the evaluation of social development see *Evaluation of Social Development Projects, Development Guidelines 5*, edited by David Marsden and Peter Oakley, published by Oxfam in 1990.)

Validation

Validation means cross-checking information from different sources to ensure consistency, and agreements between sources of information. By investing time in validation a clear picture can often be constructed based on a collection of apparently unconnected sources of information. Given the reality of development you will seldom have the luxury of carrying out all the primary, first-hand research required to cover all your information needs. Instead you will be drawing together different information, most of which will be partial; but by cross-checking, putting bits of information together, you may piece together the whole. For example, whereas it is probably impossible to survey all the child labourers in a city, it may be possible to identify information in official records, cross-check these with surveys carried out in one district then cross-check this with material collected in another district, so as to be able to estimate the figure for child workers in the city by extrapolating the numbers in the two districts to the estimated child population in the whole city.

The key principles of validation are never to take anything at face value, never to rely on one person's opinion or perception, and to cross-check the different perceptions of different actors or observers about the same fact. For example, to gauge the impact of a programme you should check the views of the beneficiaries, those not helped by the programme, the programme workers, and government officials.

Analysis is an aspect of validation, and both sides of an argument, or contrasting perceptions, should be included in the final analysis or report. The differences do not need to be resolved in the report: the resolution comes in the recommendations and conclusions at the end of the summary. Unpalatable findings or disappointing data should never be excluded from the report. For example, if a market study of exploitative middle-men shows that in fact marketing costs are very high and the level of exploitation thus relatively low, the report must show this or fail to be honest.

Pre-testing of questions and surveys or the use of pilot studies may save a great deal of time by validating the questions themselves to check whether they are relevant or useful or give the information required.

Be cautious as to the quality of official and other data; even sources such as national censuses may be designed with major faults in them (Peru census includes all children born, not those who are still alive at the time of the census, and assumes that all children registered at school do not work). In some recent work on the informal sector of the economy (See, for example, *Income Generation and the Urban Poor, Development Guidelines 4*, by Donnacadh Hurley, published by Oxfam in 1990, in which it was pointed out that official economic data did not include the contribution of the informal sector to the economy, or registered all informal sector workers as unemployed or under-employed, which obviously gives a very distorted picture of the economy and labour force.)

Be wary of those in whose interest it is to operate a policy of distortion of facts. A government could be consistently under-estimating the population of a particular region in order to understate the real number of a religious 'minority' and inflate the number of the 'majority' adherents to the official religion. A similar example was the consistent over-estimate by the Siad Barre regime of refugees in Somalia in order to attract more aid.

It may be useful to use someone for the validation exercise who was not involved in the original research design, to ensure that assumptions are questioned and that any tendency for the research to be designed to prove a preconceived but inaccurate thesis is identified. It is difficult to be totally self-validating, as it involves calling in question our basic assumptions; that is why it is advisable to use an outsider to facilitate the process.

Validation is, after all, a familiar part of our daily life. We are always cross-checking different information, for example, to compare the prices in our local shops. The difference is that when carrying out a research exercise, validation needs to be systematically and carefully built into the process at the planning stage.

After research: some crucial questions

Ethical use of information: Can the data collected be used in any way to harm the interests of those who provided it? Must access to it be restricted to protect informants? Have any informants' identities been revealed, where it would be wiser to keep them anonymous?   Who 'owns' the information? Is it clear whether the people who collected the information own it, or the subjects of the research, or the commissioning agency who paid

81

for the research? Whatever the contractual obligations of the researchers and their employers, there is also an ethical dilemma over the use of the information obtained from a 'subject' population. There is as yet little or no protection for people who may have unwittingly supplied information about their livelihood. Data protection legislation is still in its infancy.

Access to research: Traditionally a great deal of research was carried out by universities and other research centres and was in theory at least accessible to all who wished to consult the published results. Gaining access to university libraries tended to need an academic sponsor, but the intention of the researchers was to make information available through publications. Recently the trend has been increasingly towards commissioned research, and more research is now classified as confidential because it is carried out within the confines of programme cycles and refers to the individuals managing these programmes. Because of a change in the economic and political fortunes of independent researchers many of them now carry out research as consultants, reinforcing the tendency to make material the property of the commissioning agency. It is perhaps understandable that agencies will withhold information if they feel that its release could cause damage. Sometimes people will hold back from being honest if they are aware that what they write will be publicised, especially where management and decision-making processes are included in the research or evaluation being carried out. It is to be hoped that agencies seek to establish guidelines which are neither too restrictive in making information less accessible nor compromising in their openness. We need to distinguish between 'private' information relating to a programme and its personnel and information which should be in the public domain.

Report writing: You should include in the final report a section on the methodology used to collect the information; this may be a simple list of people interviewed or copies of questionnaires used. Other details which explain the process used in the data collection are useful for those checking the validity of your findings but also give guidance to others who may need to check or reassess a situation in the future.

Communicating the results: How is the information being disseminated and to whom? Different media will be appropriate to different groups; academic journals may reach a handful of people, more popularly written booklets a wider number, short newspaper style reports more still and so on. As noted above, some groups have used theatre, video, film, and radio to disseminate their findings.

Evaluating research: When the research has been completed, the original terms of reference should be reviewed to see how far the results of the research have met the original needs the terms of reference expressed. In the case of research which is essentially a programme evaluation, it may also be important to see who needs to take action on the research. This may also apply to feasibility studies.

Lessons learned: What have the different people involved in the process learned? This should not only include those commissioning and directing the research but also everyone else. For example, if interviewers were involved or the staff of a project, did they learn anything from the process of data collection and analysis? Were attempts made to explain to them what the conclusions were and how they were reached? Did they learn anything about the process of data collection itself, and the techniques involved? Furthermore was there any attempt to feed back to the groups being researched? We have seen examples where researchers/evaluators have employed methods such as popular drama to illustrate some of the findings of a research programme (see Roy Trivedy's work in Malawi, discussed in Appendix 6). Where a group is literate it is often possible to feed back the outline of a report on the spot, and of course the word processor has made it much easier to produce draft reports *in situ* rather than having to wait until they have been typed and printed.

Benefits to the community: Has the community gained any new knowledge or skills as a result of the process of research? A great deal of participatory research enables groups to review their own situation and to learn the techniques for carrying out their own reviews in the future.

Use of research: Underlining all these questions is the key one: how is the research being used? Merely to further the careers of researchers? For the internal decision making of the commissioning institution (be it government or NGO)? For action in terms of redesigning an existing development programme or initiating a new one? There are many examples around the world where there is very little feedback from research or where information is not available in the country in which the research was carried out. There are ways of making even academic material available, for example, by placing copies of reports in local university libraries; making copies of data discs available, and producing annotated bibliographies of material collected during the research.

Lastly, is there a channel for criticism or experience to feed back? If things go wrong how do project designers and managers find out about it and take action? Are the opportunities created for people at the sharp end to comment on what they are being asked to do? Are communication channels open? Has the research experience fostered a critical culture and fresh thinking among all concerned?

BIBLIOGRAPHY

Beaudoux E. et al (1990), *Supporting Development Action at Community Level: a methodological guide*, Belgium: COTA.

Casley, D.J. and Lury, D.A. (1981), *Data Collection in Developing Countries*, Oxford: Clarendon Press

Cole, R. (ed.) (1989), *Measuring Drought and Drought Impacts in Red Sea Province*, Oxford: Oxfam.

(1988) 'Participation in Evaluation', *Community Development Journal*, Oxford: Oxford University Press.

Epstein, T.S. (1988), *A Manual for Culturally Adapted Market Research in the Development Process*, Sussex: RWAL Publications.

Fernandes, W. and Tandon, R. (1981), *Participatory Research and Evaluation: Experiments in research as a process of liberation*, New Delhi: ISI.

Feurstein, M.T., (1986), *Partners in Evaluation*, London: Macmillan.

Gardner, Katy (1991) *Songs at the River's Edge: stories from a Bangladeshi Village*. (Sensitive evocation by a young European woman of living in a Muslim community as a researcher.) Virago.

International Institute for Environment and Development [IIED] *Newsletter on Rapid Rural Appraisal*.

Marsden D and Oakley P. (1990), *Evaluating Social Development Projects, Development Guidelines 5*, Oxford: Oxfam.

Nichols P. (1991), *Social Survey Methods: A fieldguide for development workers, Development Guidelines 6*, Oxford: Oxfam.

Oakley, P. (1991), *Projects with People*, Geneva: ILO.

Robertson, A.F. (1978),*Community of Strangers* (An informal description of anthropological research in Uganda.), London: Scolar Press

Trivedy, R. (1990), *Action Research in Southern Malawi*, Oxford: Oxfam.

Tina Wallace with Candida March (eds) (1991) *Changing Perceptions: writings on Gender and Development.* Oxfam.

UNICEF (1988), *Methodological Guide on Situation Analysis of Children in Especially Difficult Circumstances*, UNICEF: Bogota.

APPENDIX 1   CHECK-LIST OF QUESTIONS

Do you really need to do some research?

Who needs to know what, and why? For policy formation? To assist a decision on a grant application? To monitor or evaluate a project? To assess needs in an emergency?

Could it be that someone has already done the research you think you need?

How much time have you got? As long as you like? A year? Three months? A week? A day?

How much will it cost to find out? Will a specific level of accurate research justify a relatively large expenditure? If you are being asked to spend £5,000, is it worth £250 of research to make a reasoned decision?

Have you the staff you need? Do you need expertise? Can local people undertake some or all of the research? Can you train up some helpers in the time available?

Have you consulted local people? How far does the proposed research take account of local perceptions of real-world problems? Is this the research the local community thinks it needs? Will you check with them at each main phase?

Will your research arouse local expectations? Is it clear to the community why this research is being done? Are people expecting miracles, or major commitments, just because some questions are being asked? Will their expectations skew the findings?

Have you thought about possible bias? Gender bias? Class bias? Locational bias? Ethnicity? Religion?

What is the research unit? A region? A village? A cluster of settlements? A category of people, such as landless labourers? Individuals? Households? How is the unit defined and bounded? Are there any 'missing persons' (labour migrants, herders)?

What about time? Will you take a snapshot, or must you follow a process over a period of months? Will the research be affected by the data having to be gathered over a period of several months, or in a particular season?

Will you need to sample a large population, or is it practical to deal with everyone? What kind of sample makes most sense?

One method or several? Is there an ideal research method to meet your needs, or do you need to combine several? What matters most - predictive accuracy, because it will affect expenditure, or the quality of the insights? The need to maintain good rapport with a vulnerable group?

Can existing sources meet your needs? Is there a national census with data on your region? Has a department of local government tried to answer these particular questions?

Is your research vulnerable to informant bias? Have you become the intellectual prisoner of any particular section of local opinion? Have you any cross-checking procedures to help in validation?

Can you, should you, use a sample survey or questionnaire?

What about participant observation? Have you the time to do this? Has someone already done it for you? Is there an experienced anthropologist or rural sociologist who knows this region, speaks the language, and can get your questions answered in a few weeks' intensive work?

Rapid Rural Appraisal? Should you field a team of specialists, who will consult relevant literature, then work flexibly with local people and present their provisional findings to them, and to you, in a series of workshops?

Have you really taken advantage of local knowledge, local memories, local skills? They have had a lot of experience in surviving and adapting - is your research giving that experience full weight?

Has the research got back to the people it was meant to help?

APPENDIX 2 QUESTIONNAIRE DESIGN

We assume that the purpose is to assess community interest in a local person running a small mini-bus service to surrounding market towns. If community interest is strong enough, there might be a case for making a loan to the future operator. The two questionnaires are obviously not complete - merely initial sections tackling obvious issues.

A poorly designed questionnaire

Q1 Do you travel a lot outside the village?

(The interviewer has jumped straight into the task without a word of explanation or introduction. This is bound to seem abrupt, if not rude. The question itself is a very vague ques tion. What is 'a lot', and what will be learned from the answer, whether it is 'yes' or 'no'?)

Q2 Would you travel more if there were cheap transport?

(Another vague question, and it is hypothetical, as well. It invites the answer 'yes' and little more.)

Q3 How do you travel?

(This question will encourage a very general answer, and possibly some confusion. If the listener is thinking about the next village, one kind of answer will emerge; but if they are thinking of a market town 50 kilometres away, then another will apply.)

Q4 When do you travel?

(Although this question looks specific, it can elicit all kinds of answers: 'When I have to.' 'When someone offers me a lift.' 'When I have something to sell.' 'When I must buy something.' 'If a child is sick.' The question merges times, and motives in the word 'when' and gives no clue as to which kind of answer is intended.)

Q5 Who else in your household also travels outside the village?

(As we suggested in the main text, it is much better to ask each member of the household about their actual behaviour, separately. The only excuse for a question in this form would be a drastic shortage of time and money, and it is possible that a male household head would give answers about his wife or children which carried implications about his status and authority, and could not necessarily be a reli able guide to what really happens, or what other family members would like.)

A more thoughtfully designed questionnaire

Introduction: Hello. My name is X...... and I have been invited to your community by the mayor. I am trying to understand about how much the people here travel outside the village, and some related things. Could you please spare me a little time - about 15 minutes? I am asking people from every house in the village. There are no right or wrong answers to the questions, and you should not find it at all difficult to reply because they are all things you know about from your daily life.

(These introductory remarks inform the interviewee exactly what is going on and should make them feel relaxed and unthreatened.)

Q1 In the last 12 months, you may have travelled outside the vil lage. I want to write down all the times you did this, and for what purposes, starting with the most recent trip.

A 1   the place ....the reasons...................

A 2   the place..................the reasons...................

A 3   the place...................the reasons...................

A 4   the place...................the reasons...................

A 5   the place...................the reasons...................

(continue on separate sheet if necessary)

(By choosing actual, recent behaviour, and by eliciting an open-ended number of examples, this question and the following questions, avoid the vague generalities which might have resulted from the first questionnaire.)

Q2 When you travelled to (place, from A1) how did you travel?

Tick one of the following:

on foot ❑   on an animal ❑

by bicycle ❑   by motorbike/moped ❑

in a lorry ❑   in a mini-bus ❑

in a large bus ❑ in a car ❑

other [specify]..

(Repeat with all the answers from Q 1.)

Q3 How much did it cost to travel to (place from A1)
(Repeat for all answers to Q1.)

Q4 How much is it worth to you to be able to go once a week
to the town of XYZ, and come back the same day?

A1 not more than 50 pesos
A2 from 55-75 pesos?
A3 from 80-100 pesos?
A4 from 105-120 pesos?
A5 from 125-150 pesos?

(This question is hypothetical, and so suspect. It would need
to be checked against actual prices being paid, either in this
community or in a similar one.)

APPENDIX 3 SOME HIGH-TECH, HIGH-COST RESEARCH METHODS

You are unlikely to employ these methods directly in a 'hands-on' sense in project research because they require special skills, or costly equipment. But it is useful to know they exist, and how their results might be exploited by you if you can buy them in 'off the shelf'.

Aerial/satellite photographs: the use of aerial photos and satellite photos and images can help give a view on a large scale, not only for the more obvious physical features of an area, but can also allow estimates to be made of population and livestock densities. They can also be used for city mapping; this may be of particular importance given the delay in incorporating new slum/squatter settlements in many city maps. Of course, such large-scale pictures will not help you to piece together social relationships but it will give you access to crude numbers which can then be supplemented by on the ground validation.

Off-the-shelf data: A great deal of material is often available 'off the shelf' from large agencies and can be obtained free of charge or at low cost. Although one needs to be aware that sometimes there may be security sensitivities about access to material (and for this reason many countries locate maps and aerial photos in the military institutes rather than civilian).

Time comparisons: Geographic information may enable comparisons across time as even in countries with a weak administrative infrastructure on the ground it may be possible to find photographic and other information. For example, material was found from the 1960s which allowed comparisons of *wadis* in Sudan with the present day. Other land use patterns can be established for which oral traditions may be inaccurate and administrative records unavailable, especially in 'marginal areas' such as arid zones or rain forests.

Mapping changes: mapping can also be useful in tracing the development of cities especially where the administrative boundaries failed to recognise or keep abreast with growth, a problem commonly encountered in fast-growing Third World cities, whose administrative capabilities are over-stretched.

You can use this material for historical comparison of settlements, land use, and land use changes, true rates of desertification, etc., and to resolve issues otherwise difficult to verify. Around Picchis Palcazu in the central Peruvian jungle, the government claimed there were no settlements but overflying confirmed a considerable number (3,500 colonist and 3,500 tribal people) of people settled in the valley and involved in agriculture; in Sudan, maps were used to establish whether certain areas were suffering drought or not, and whether this was exceptional or normal to the area.

There is a danger with all technology that it can mystify rather than illuminate and for this reason it is not used even when it could supply crucial information. However, we would again stress the need for validation on the ground to cross-check the material gathered at a macro level. For example, a settlement may be identified through aerial photos, but on a follow-up visit we may find that many of the dwellings have been abandoned.

Geographic systems are not a substitute for social research. They may identify how many animals are grazing in an area, but will not show who owns them, how they are used, or where they are sold. You need also to be aware of seasonal differences, especially as some techniques may only be utilised at certain times of the year (aerial photos are taken when flying conditions are good and visibility clear).

Technology is a good servant but a poor master. Its sales staff and enthusiasts will hard-sell it, because they stand to profit from it, or are caught up in its exciting capabilities. You should not be seduced into thinking hi-tech systems can resolve all your problems, but conversely there is little gain in making life difficult by refusing to use computers, aerial photography or any other technical process if they can help you do your work better, or with less effort for the same quality of results.

Geographic information systems: This is the generic name for satellite photography used in conjunction with computers and their graphic display systems in the understanding of phenomena distributed on the earth's surface i.e. physical rather than social characteristics. The GIS is a computerised system for the specification, acquisition, storage, retrieval and manipulation of data in a defined physical area, for example a county or district. The principle task of a GIS is to make many and diverse forms of data comprehensible and to elicit patterns and relationships between variables where they exist. Typical data sources that are used are soil surveys, air photos, landsat images, topographic and thematic maps, tabular data, and almost any form of survey of other features in the area. A vast range of material could be incorporated such as land use, land cover analysis, farm size, field size, livestock population, agricultural production, vegetation type and density, farm buildings, grain stores, human population, malnutrition rates, and many others. There is no limit in theory to the number of variables that may be used as long as they relate to the defined target area.

The advantage of the GIS over manual records is that all of the above sources of data and different variables may be combined to produce new classifications of the space or area and can be examined in relationship to other variables. The results can be expressed in a report, graphical, cartographical or statistical form. The map is the most easily understood and common product of a GIS. The GIS is composed of both hardware and software. The hardware is usually a minicomputer, a digitising table, a pen plotter, a dot matrix printer and a high resolution monitor or screen. Sometimes a tape drive is included for reading tapes of landsat satellite images for use as a base map and data source for the GIS. A digitising table is used to do two things: enter the area of the earth to be studied and identify and assign values to discrete entities. The digitising table attached to the computer is really an electronic table of defined space composed of thousands of tiny sensors. Typically the base map is taped to the top of the table and identified as occupying such and such a space. A small digitising puck is used to locate points and areas on the map on the digitising table and enter them onto the computer. The whole thing is like an electronic tracing paper. There are many software packages available for the analysis of spatial data. A fully equipped system is likely to cost in the region of more than 20.000 sterling, and will require skilled staff to use it.

APPENDIX 4 LOGICAL FRAMEWORK ANALYSIS

Logical framework analysis (LFA) is also known as Project Framework Analysis. LFA was first developed in the US but has been adopted and modified by a number of governmental agencies, and increasingly by NGOs. Many governmental co-funding donor agencies now encourage NGOs to use LFA in preparing their project proposals and reports. As noted in the Introduction to this book, LFA is not really a research method but a way of ordering information. The names may be different but the basic approaches are similar in that they clearly relate to 'projects' and all assume that these are designed to effect a positive change in the lives of people. LFA is based on a relatively simple matrix whereby objectives are matched to project activities and assessed in terms of inputs (resources utilised) and outputs (benefits). These are then measured by previously agreed indicators in the light of the risks and assumptions made by the project planners. An illustrative sketch of a LFA matrix is given below.

The proponents of LFA argue that it brings together key statements and information in one document and ensures that project objectives are clearly spelt out. It enables people to relate project actions to project purposes and goals, as well as the resources utilised and outputs attained. It provides a basis for further monitoring and evaluation and is a flexible system, which can be adapted to suit various purposes.

However, critics are unhappy about the dominance of LFA in many agencies because they feel that the system can be very inflexible in that it can force people to think in terms of easily quantifiable and rigidly defined categories. They argue that development workers find themselves being obliged to summarise complex ideas and social relationships into meaningless phrases. In addition, they are expected to quantify the unquantifiable, or measure major social changes and movements.

A further criticism is that LFA is too project-centred, and forces research, reporting, and evaluations unnecessarily into the framework of projects. Many people argue that projects in themselves are merely short, artificially created episodes imposed on the social processes through which people are living.

ZOPP: ZOPP (Target Oriented Project Planning) was developed in Germany in the early 1980s. It is based on LFA, with certain additional elements. These are, an emphasis on the team approach to project planning, and a recognition of the importance of the pre-planning research and survey work required to ensure that problems re properly identified and that their causes and effects are related to the real experiences and needs of individuals and groups of people. These problems, it is said, can then become the basis for agreeing project objectives.

The advocates of ZOPP have also relied on the use of visual aids such as wall charts for group meetings involved in activities of planning or monitoring activities. People are encouraged to contribute by writing their ideas on cards which are added to the wall-chart, which may be based on a LFA matrix.

Typical LFA Matrix (based on one used by the British ODA)

	Indicators	Measurement (Means)	Assumptions and Risks
Main Objectives			
Short-term Objectives			
Outputs			
Inputs			

APPENDIX 5 WOMEN AND EVALUATION

(This paper, by Frances Rubin, was originally published in *Changing Perceptions: Writings on gender and Development*, published by Oxfam in 1991. It gives a first-hand account of some of the problems that may be encountered in attemping to involve women in research projects.)

It is now nearly two years since I first coordinated an Oxfam Country Programme Review. The exercise gave plenty of food for thought about the difficulties that women can face in development work, and particularly in the process of evaluation. This note is anecdotal, but may illustrate some of the problems and give pointers to solutions, or at least steps that need to be taken to address the danger of excluding women from important moments of decision making.

Terms of reference

One of the first tasks to be completed was the drafting of the terms of reference (TOR) for the review in collaboration with the Country Representative. The programme staff had voiced concern about how to tackle gender questions within their work, and were trying to develop a country strategy where 'gender' was seen as an important issue. Following consultation with a number of colleagues, 'gender questions' were written into many aspects of the TOR. There was quite a strong reaction to this. Many people felt that such explicit mention of gender issues suggested that nobody, including consultants who might be contracted, were aware of gender issues. Because of these strong feeling the TOR were modified but remained explicit in terms of briefing the evaluation team members that gender issues were to be treated in an integral way throughout the evaluation. Above all, gender was not to be treated as a discrete issue in a separate chapter.

Contracting of consultants

At one time in the course of looking for members of the evaluation team it seemed possible that they might all be women. This raised reactions of alarm among some who suggested that an all women team might not be balanced. For how many years has Oxfam used all male teams without feeling concerned? At the end of the day the evaluation team was composed of two men and three women. At times they split up into different groups but these were always mixed.

Field visits

Even though gender was recognised as a central issue and there were always women in the visiting teams, we still encountered considerable difficulties in actually meeting women and hearing their views.

In a number of situations the male members of the team explained with confidence what women thought on a number of issues. To give one example, they explained that women could not participate in training courses because they needed to stay at home to look after the domestic affairs of the household. However, when we spoke directly with women, the women outlined various strategies that would enable them to leave their families and community, and attend meetings they saw as relevant.

On one particular day we were carrying out a programme of visits that had been organised by the village leaders. We asked if we (the visiting Oxfam team) could split up into two groups, so that the women on the team could talk separately to the women in the village. Since this was not on the agenda it took quite an effort to organise, and we were continually interrupted by people who wanted us to hurry so that we could rejoin the 'main' delegation.

Another time, I was reading the notes in the file, as we were on our way to meet a women's group. In one of the tour reports it was clearly stated on which days it was inappropriate to visit if you wanted to talk to the women — because the women were preparing for, and selling in, the market. Yet we found ourselves *en route* to this town precisely on market day! This happened again in another small community, where there was a very low turn out of women because they were all busy preparing manioc loaves for the market on the following day.

On our last project visit, committee members of a health post began to assemble for the customary discussion. One by one the com-mittee members were introduced. There was one women member. Her name was read out 'Citoyenne (treasurer) — present.' 'Present?' I asked, 'but where?' The treasurer then popped her head into the inner circle of the crowd, bowed and disappeared.

After the round of introductions was complete I asked why the citoyenne who was present in the village was not participating in the meeting? The reason for her absence was that she was busy preparing lunch for the delegation. We politely suggested that she should be present at the discussions. She appeared, and in the course of the debates raised a number of issues of importance: issues related to the management and safekeeping of the finances that had been entrusted to her, as well as health issues that were of specific importance to the female members of the community, and which had not been raised by the other members present.

A plate of cold peanuts was passed round instead of a lovely meal: we had passed up on some culinary delights but we had enabled the treasurer to raise some important questions for the community; had she not been in the meeting these issues would not have been brought to Oxfam's notice.

Conclusion

It must be a rule that the TOR of all evaluations include gender as an integral part; that, except in very specific circumstances, there should be mixed evaluation teams and that, however difficult it continues to be, women evaluators must ensure that they get the opportunity to talk to women on their own.

APPENDIX 6 ACTION RESEARCH PROGRAMME — THE METHODS AND ARPROACH

(This is an extract from a paper by Roy Trivedy, *Action Research in Southern Malawi*, published by Oxfam in 1990. It describes the methods employed in research undertaken for Oxfam in Mulanje District, during 1987 and 1988. The aims of the research were threefold. Firstly, to identify and explore in detail the development problems and priorities of the rural communities in Mulanje District. In particular, the research sought to discover the problems and priorities of some of the most vulnerable groups of people. Secondly, to identify and explore possible solutions to these problems and priorities, and thirdly, to make recommendations to Oxfam on its future role in Malawi.)

The approach of the ARP can be broadly divided into three main stages. The preliminary stage, lasting from mid–August until the end of October, included the formulation of the basic approach, selection of villages, and selection and initial training of the research assistants. The second stage, 'fieldwork', lasted for four months from the beginning of November 1987 until the end of February 1988. Finally, the third stage 'post fieldwork', has included circulating a summary of our findings as well as consulting with various groups of people about the validity of our findings and the question of how Oxfam could follow up and build on the work of the ARP. In this section we will provide a more detailed account of each of these stages.

The preliminary stage

This began with the Development Adviser conducting a literature review to find out:

what had been written about rural poverty in Malawi;
what methods had been used in conducting research on similar themes; and

specific details about Mulanje District which could be useful for the ARP.

The literature review revealed a number of interesting things. Firstly, we found that there was very little written specifically on rural poverty in Malawi. Although a number of writers had dealt with many closely related subjects, including malnutrition and food availability, the effectiveness of agricultural extension, women's and smallholders' participation in agricultural development, and the role of income–generating activities in rural areas, we found very little literature which had attempted to deal with the issue of rural poverty in any comprehensive manner. Secondly, we found that, with few exceptions, almost all of the research which had been carried out in Malawi on the above mentioned themes had utilised formal, structured questionnaires as an essential part of their methods. Whilst formal structured questionnaires do have certain advantages over more 'open–ended' research methods, it was felt that if we were genuinely to try to find out from the rural poor themselves how they define their needs and priorities, it would be more appropriate to use other research methods. Apart from the literature survey, another factor which assisted us in formulating the research methods was our initial discussions with several key people in the area including staff at the District Commissioner's office and at the Rural Development Projects at Mulanje and Phalombe. These discussions confirmed our view that if structured questionnaires were used as part of the research methods then it would prove extremely difficult for us to gain any further insights beyond what was already known on the problems and priorities of the poor, let alone to increase people's awareness ofthese.

By mid–September we had begun to formulate an outline of the research methods which we felt would be appropriate. We proposed to have six Malawian research assistants staying in six villages for a period of approximately four months from November to February 1988. Although it would have been interesting to employ more research assistants and thereby work in more than six villages in the District, we felt that this would have been detrimental in terms of the quality of support and supervision that the Development Adviser would be able to provide. We hoped to employ an equal number of female and male researchers and wanted to try to ensure that the researchers were of different ages. The six villages which would be chosen were to be well spread geographically so that the findings would provide a fair indication of the problems and priorities of people in the District as a whole (see below on village selection). A variety of factors influenced the decision to do the fieldwork for a period of four months. Firstly, if we were to be able to make recommendations to Oxfam by July/August of 1988, we felt it would be problematic to extend the field work much beyond March. Although the initial plans envisaged a four–month period of fieldwork, the decision about whether it might be appropriate to extend the fieldwork for a further month, until the end of March, was left open. Secondly, it was felt that the four–month period November to February would roughly coincide with the peak agricultural period for farmers and also the period of 'annual maximum stress' for people, in terms of food availability and health–related problems. Much of the research in Malawi, as elsewhere, has been done during the dry season, and by doing the fieldwork during the rainy season, we were aware of this being a 'seasonal reversal'. Although we were aware that there was a danger that many farmers would be 'too busy' in their fields to talk with the researchers, we felt that the advantages of doing the research during this period outweighed this. We felt that the main advantage was that seasonal factors would enable the researchers to identify the most vulnerable groups of people much more easily. In addition the researchers themselves would learn a lot about rural life just as a result of having experienced life in the villages during the rainy season, when many of the problems faced by rural people are most acute.

During their stay in the villages the researchers were to conduct a 'listening survey'. The idea was that the researchers would begin by establishing trust and equality with villagers. Thereafter they would be engaged in listening to people in dif-

102

ferent situations, at work, at the market, during leisure activities, in their homes, etc. At the same time as listening to people, the researchers were to make observations about village life and also informally talk with people. By using these methods it was felt that we were more likely to be able to find out from people themselves about their problems and priorities. A crucial element of the exercise was that the researchers were to make it clear from the beginning that they were there to learn from the villagers about rural life, what problems confront people, how people cope with these and what people's own priorities are.

One issue which we were very aware of, concerned the possibility that our work might raise people's expectations. Having explained their problems/priorities to the researchers, it was felt that people might then expect the researchers or the Government or perhaps even Oxfam, to provide 'solutions'. We discussed this issue at length in our initial training session and also in many of the ongoing training sessions. We felt that it was crucial to explain the purpose of the research to villagers clearly from the beginning so that no false expectations were created. This was felt to be of such importance that part of the initial training session specifically involved each researcher practising explaining the purpose of the research in Chichewa in front of other people, so that any ideas which could raise expectations would be omitted. It was also felt that we should explain to people that ultimately the research aimed to assist the Government of Malawi and other agencies to improve 'development planning' in the country. Hence, although the villagers themselves would not immediately gain anything as a result of the research, it was hoped that in the longer term the District as a whole would benefit through better development planning. (See also fieldwork part of this Section.)

To assist the researchers a set of broad 'guidelines' were prepared. These were in the form of a set of questions covering a number of specific areas of interest for the study, including social organisation, land constraints, agricultural extension/advice and training, credit/loans, labour supply, irrigation, soil conservation, livestock, forestry, off–farm income and ideas for income generation, health/illness, water and sanitation, nutrition, patterns of work, exchanges and transfers, and income/expenditure. It was pointed out to the researchers that the guidelines were not exhaustive but merely sought to outline some of the types of information which it would be useful to find out, particularly when villagers themselves raised specific subjects as priority/problem areas. Moreover, it was made clear that the guidelines were not to preclude the researchers from collecting information on other areas which villagers themselves prioritised. The researchers were informed that the guidelines were not to be interpreted as a rigid list of information which had to be collected. The purpose and aims of the guidelines were discussed extensively during the initial training session and the guidelines were revised and reformulated in subsequent meetings of the team.

A final point concerning the research methods was that the field work was divided into two parts. In the first part, lasting approximately six to eight weeks, the researchers were to attempt to build up a general picture of the problems and priorities of the village as a whole and the extent to which existing service provisions met or failed to meet these needs. In addition, during this period, the researchers were to identify some of the most vulnerable groups of people in their village, and this meant that they had to ensure that they met every person in their village. The main emphasis of the first part of the research was on the researchers establishing a relationship of equality and trust with villagers; without this we felt that the second stage of the research would be extremely difficult and probably unsuccessful. In the second part of the fieldwork, we focused much more closely on the more disadvantaged members of the communities in order to try to identify their problems and priorities. By using this method we felt that we were more likely to be able to find out the priorities of the poorest and most vulnerable groups without stigmatising these groups. [Note: We are indebted to PHAM (Private Hospital Association of Malawi) Primary Health Care experiences for making us aware of this factor. We also felt that it would have been impossible for us to gain any significant insights into the issues of intra–household and gender inequalities without the researchers first building up a sufficient level of trust with each of the communities as a whole. The other advantage of this approach concerns the question of the unit of analysis in this type of research. By focusing initially on wider social relations and not only on 'the household' we felt that we were more likely to be able to distinguish between the 'idealised family forms and the reality of family structures'.]

Having decided on the methods to be used, the next stage involved selecting the six villages. We used three main criteria for the selection of the villages. Firstly, we felt that since only one researcher would be based in each village the size of the village, particularly in terms of population, had to be one determining factor in our choice. In this respect we felt that it would be unrealistic to expect the researchers to do the work effectively if the population of the village exceeded 250–300 people. Unfortunately, the only data available at the time on the population of villages in the District was from the Census of 1977. Since this was out of date, we estimated that the population of each village would probably have grown by approximately 3 per cent each year since 1977. On the basis of these very rough figures we shortlisted 28 possible villages for the research. A second criterion used was that the villages should be geographically well spread. In this respect the literature survey and our discussions with people in the District proved useful. Since we were already aware of some locally specific problems in the District, we felt that by having a good geographical spread of villages we were more likely to be able to build up a picture of the problems and priorities of people in Mulanje as a whole. A third set of criteria which was used was what may be described as essential practicalities. These included:

that the selected villages had to be accessible with a four–wheel–drive vehicle throughout the rainy season (although we were also conscious of trying to avoid villages which were unrepresentatively near to main roads or other main service provisions); and

that some accommodation was available which could be rented for the four–month period in the selected villages. In this respect we were conscious that the hired accommodation should be representative of housing conditions in the village generally, and that no special favours were made available which would make the researchers' experiences unrepresentative of life in the village.

During late September and early October, 18 short–listedvillages were visited in order to try to assess which villages fitted the criteria and would be suitable for the work. The visits were made with accompanying staff from either the Rural Development Projects or Community Development or other service providers. The visits enabled the Development Adviser to learn more, through the discussions with accompanying staff, as well as people in each of the villages especially the 'Village Headmen'. The final selection of the six villages was done after consultation with the DC's office in Mulanje, Blantyre ADD officials, the RDP staff and Louis Msukwa. The DC's office agreed to notify the Village Headmen in each of the six villages, as well as local party officials, so that we could start the fieldwork at the beginning of November.

The next stage of the work involved the selection and training of the research assistants. In mid–October, Louis Msukwa and the Development Adviser interviewed seven candidates for the research assistant posts. The candidates, three women and four men, had all been educated to degree or diploma level. Five of them had previous research experience, although this had mainly involved questionnaire–based research. Two of the candidates were recent graduates. Of the seven, four (the three women and one man) had agriculture–related qualifications, the remaining three had social science backgrounds.

In terms of their ages we were not wholly successful in being able to attract people in different age ranges. Six of the candidates were in their mid–twenties, the seventh was in his early forties. We invited all seven candidates to attend the initial training sessions during which we hoped to assess the suitability of each candidate and choose six people to do the village–based work. It was hoped that the remaining candidate would perhaps be able to assist the Development Adviser either on a temporary or part–time basis.

The initial training session prior to the fieldwork lasted just over a week and was led by Louis Msukwa, Percy Kantunda of PHAM (one of Oxfam's partners in Malawi), and myself. Several factors were instrumental in determining the length of the initial training course. It was recognised that the validity of our findings ultimately depended on the level of awareness and sensitivity of the researchers, and that they had little experience of using the research methods outlined above. At the same time, however, we were keen to try to ensure that the researchers were settled in the villages prior to the start of the rains. After much thought we decided that having just over a week of initial training, followed by regular ongoing training/discussion meetings every two to three weeks during the fieldwork, would possibly be the best solution. In addition to our regular two– to three–weekly meetings, a two–day refresher training course was arranged mid–way through the fieldwork period in January.

As part of the background to the initial training session some reading material was distributed which the researchers were expected to read and which the group as a whole later discussed. The reading material included the Oxfam Country Review as well as material focusing on rural poverty and the problems of investigating this. The aim of distributing this material and discussing it was both to enable the Development Adviser to assess the researchers' awareness of rural poverty and also to increase the group's awareness of some of the problems we were likely to face during the fieldwork.

Although there were a number of themes which we had to cover in the initial training session, we did not attempt to follow a rigid pre–determined agenda. The session began with a very open discussion about development policy in Malawi in the post–independence period. This discussion was led by Percy Kantunda and the Development Adviser. By using some of the techniques developed by PHAM, namely by raising a series of questions and issues for discussion, we were able to begin thinking about how certain groups of people had been by–passed in the Country's development efforts. The discussion then moved on to the issue of which groups could be considered to be 'at risk' and how these could be identified. Part of this discussion centred on the crucial issues of the accessibility of services for the most vulnerable groups and the relevance of these services to the needs of these groups. At this stage the group discussed how services could be made more accessible and relevant to the needs of the most vulnerable groups. The group then began to realise that a prerequisite for this to take place was that service providers may often need to change and be willing to listen and learn from the most vulnerable groups. For this to become a reality, the group concluded that a relationship of trust and equality had to be established between 'service providers' and those for whom the services were meant. We then concretised these discussions by brain–storming on some techniques and methods which could be used to build up trust and equality. For this part of the course, we were able to use some of the material from the *Training for Transformation* manuals, as well as adding our own life experiences. This part of the training took up almost the whole of the first two days.

On the third day we discussed the aims of the research and the methods (including the guidelines) that we would be using in the context of what we had learnt earlier. This was followed by Louis Msukwa leading a discussion on development planning and policy in Malawi which tied together many of the themes which we had discussed. This discussion drew together the links between different sectors of the economy such as health, education and agriculture. Louis Msukwa also provided us with a lot of background information about the District, as well as drawing our attention to some of the problems we were likely to face in the fieldwork. [Note: This included discussion about village power structures, the role of local party officials, Village Headmen, traditional healers, etc.] We discussed at some length how we should introduce ourselves to villagers and how to explain the purpose and aims of the research without raising people's expectations.

The final one–and–a–half days were spent discussing ways in which our 'listening skills' could be improved, as well as talking about some of the practical arrangements, including support and supervision arrangements and recording procedures.

At the end of the training week a decision had to be made about which of the seven candidates would be left out of the work in the villages. This decision was made easier by the fact that one of the women candidates informed us that there was a strong possibility that she would not be able to work for the full four–month period. As a result we were left with four men (Mike Chibwana, Jackson Chimowa, William Chinkhadze and Henry Mchenga) and two women (Grace Kamwendo and Chimango Mkandawire). Each researcher was assigned to one of the selected villages. By the end of October we were ready to begin the field work.

Fieldwork

Despite all the preparations, our entry to some of the villages was not without problems. In the Phalombe part of the District, in two of the three selected villages (Nantapo and Ligola) there were no problems. The Village Headman and party officials had received notification of our arrival from the DC's office and were awaiting us. In the third village, where Mike Chibwana was to stay, we encountered problems in that the village leaders were unable to find suitable accommodation. We were eventually able to place Mike at Mmora village, a few miles away from the village which had originally been selected. In the Mulanje RDP area the situation was even more complicated. We found that only in one of the three villages (Misomali) were local officials expecting us. In the other two villages the authorities had not received notification from the DC's office and so we decided that it would be advisable to go back to the DC's office, ensure that local officials were notified, and return the following week. Again, lack of accommodation proved to be a problem in one of the villages. Fortunately, there was another suitable village which had originally been visited during the village selection. Hence, after making appropriate arrangements, it was agreed that we should work in that village. By the second week in November we had begun the research in the following villages; Ligola (Grace Kamwendo), Nantapo (Jackson Chimowa), Mmora (Mike Chibwana), Murotho (Henry Mchenga), Chilembwe (Chimango Mkandawire) and Misomali (William Chinkhadze).

During the first month of fieldwork, the researchers were engaged in explaining the purpose and aims of the research and introducing themselves to all the members of their village. This could perhaps have been made easier if the researchers had been able to talk to the village members in a general meeting called by the Village Headman. However, during the planting season public meetings in the villages are not encouraged by party officials because it is felt that this draws people away from their fields. In any case, in our discussions during the training we had agreed that the researchers should not ask for any special meetings to be called on their behalf. This meant that in order to meet everybody in their village the researchers had to frequent the places where groups of villagers often met. This included meetings at the water–collection points, at the market, in tea rooms and occasionally bars, accompanying people to their fields and on their way to collect firewood. At the same time the researchers visited each household in their village to ensure that no–one was left out and that every person in the village knew who the researcher was and his/her purpose in the village. We were conscious that all of this should be done with as little disruption of 'normal village life' as possible and that the researchers should not draw unnecessary attention to themselves. At this stage the researchers were mainly engaged in observing village life and listening to people.

Throughout the fieldwork period one thing which we tried to do was to cross–check a lot of the information that was collected. Whenever possible the researchers were asked to cross–check information in three different ways, a process known as 'triangulation'. For example, we were often told by individuals about the size of their landholdings. Whenever possible the researchers themselves would visit the garden and try to estimate the size themselves (the researchers with an agricultural background were generally better at this); in addition, comparisons were made with estimates of the landholding sizes of other villagers, and in some cases where Farm Assistants visited the village, the researcher would ask their opinion of the size of a particular field. By using the triangulation method, we felt that we were likely to get reliable information, particularly on things like prices of products bought and sold by private traders, *ganyu* rates, and farmers' yields of crops for the previous years. [Note: This method was also used to check information given by particular members of households. for example, initially we found that in some cases the male household head claimed that the household had enough food for their requirements throughout the year; later, through observation and by talking with the women household members, we established that in fact this was not the case.]

Throughout the fieldwork, part of the Development Adviser's role was to provide support and supervision for the researchers. During the first six to seven weeks of the work this meant visiting each of the researchers twice a week, although later the frequency of the visits was reduced to once a week. During these visits we discussed what had been happening in the village as well as any problems encountered in the research work. In some cases we were joined at these meetings by the Village Headman or other members of the village, so that if any problems had emerged from their side, these could be discussed. During many of these visits the Development Adviser was accompanied by some of the service providers from the RDP offices, the Community Development Office or from the District Social Welfare office.

In addition to these meetings, throughout the fieldwork period we met as a group, with all the researchers as well as Louis Msukwa (on several occasions), every two to three weeks for one day, when we discussed our findings as well as preparing a rough work schedule for the next few weeks. These meetings were particularly useful because they enabled each researcher to talk about his or her experiences and findings, any problems encountered and how they had sought to deal with these, and to listen to the experiences of the others and compare their own.

Despite all our efforts to try to ensure that people's expectations were not raised, just by our presence in their villages we found that in some cases people approached the researchers thinking they could somehow provide 'solutions' to their problems. Whenever we were faced with these situations our response was always to make it clear that we were unable to provide such 'solutions' but that we were willing and committed to work with people in searching for possible solutions. Throughout the research we were careful to encourage people to think about solutions to their problems which they could manage themselves. In this way we felt that we could enable people to take more control over their own lives.

One area in which it was felt the researchers needed additional training was gender awareness. On the recommendation of Oxfam's Regional Representative we therefore arranged a two–day refresher/training course in January in which we concentrated on gender as a development issue. For this training session we used materials from Oxfam's Gender and Development Unit as a basis for discussion. We also invited the Women's Officers from Blantyre ADD and Mulanje RDP to these sessions.

During the second stage of the fieldwork, once each of the researchers had identified some of the most vulnerable households in their village, the researchers spent much more of their time with these households. It was at this stage that we were able to find out much more about intra–household inequalities, since the researchers spent a lot of their time talking with different members of the households.

The decision about whether we should extend the fieldwork beyond the four months which had initially been envisaged was made at the beginning of February. The two women researchers had been offered full–time employment which they were due to start in early March and so it would not have been possible for us to continue working in Ligola or Chilembwe. The other factor which was instrumental in our decision not to extend the field-work was that we felt we would already have a good indication of how much was likely to be harvested by most vulnerable groups and the proportion of the produce which was likely to be consumed prior to the harvest. In view of this we decided not to extend the fieldwork beyond the end of February.

Post–fieldwork

Throughout the four–month fieldwork period we made a con-scious effort to keep people in the villages, including Village Headmen and party officials, informed about our findings in their own villages. In addition, officials at the DC's office, the RDP's, Blantyre ADD, and other local officials in Mulanje were regularly informed about our overall findings. At the beginning of February we arranged a meeting with the DDC officials in Mulanje to inform them of our findings, to find out from them if there was any additional information we should try to ascertain, and to get DDC officials thinking about some of the ways in which we could build on the work of the ARP.

In March the first summary report of our overall findings was produced and this was circulated to OPC, various Ministries, Blantyre ADD, officials in Mulanje, as well as other interested parties. The main aim of this was to find out whether the find-ings were valid and to stimulate discussion and thought about how we could seek to address the problems and priorities which had been identified. During this process of consultation we were able to get comments, ideas and suggestions from a variety of sources and much of April and May was spent following these up.

In addition to this, we felt that we owed a duty to go back to each of the villages and inform people about our findings for the District as a whole. We also tried to find out from them whether they felt the findings were accurate (were there things that we had missed out or things which had been given too little or too much emphasis). This process of consultation was seen as another opportunity for us to learn from the villagers but also to raise people's awareness of their own situation and in this way to enable them to take more control of their own lives. Ideally, we would have liked each of the researchers to go back to their villages and spend a few days there during which time they could inform/consult with everyone. Unfortunately, we were unable to do this because four of the researchers had started work with other organisations and were unable to take time off work. Instead, each researcher went back to their village, and spent three to four hours there, during which they briefed a meeting of the village as a whole, as well as following this up by talking with smaller groups of people. In many respects this was not ideal, since the most vulnerable groups of people generally do not attend meetings, and when they do they are often unable to speak in public. In most cases, however, we found that because the researchers had worked particularly closely with the most vulnerable groups these were well–represented at the meetings and the researchers were able to talk with these members of the community informally after the meeting. The numbers of people attending each of the meetings varied between 50 and 90–100 adults, plus children. Women were well–represented at the meetings and in several villages outnumbered the men at the meetings. In one of the villages (Misomali) we were able to involve the Theatre for Development Group. They accompanied us to the village and performed a short series of sketches involving the community, based on our findings on the theme of apathy and its links with agriculture, health and education in the village. We found this to be an extremely useful medium of getting many more people actively involved in the process of consultation. Unfortunately, the 'Theatre for Development Group were unable to accompany us to the other villages. Nevertheless, the scope for 'animation' work in the villages through a group such as the Theatre for Development was very apparent.

The process of consultation at the village level was particularly useful in terms of our findings. It enabled us to incorporate some additional factors in the draft of the final report. Another part of the consultation process before the final report was pre-

114

pared was a workshop held in late July. The workshop was attended by Government Officials, local service providers from Mulanje, as well as NGOs and other interested parties, and we were able to discuss the findings and recommendations.

INDEX